THE MOMENT TO SHOUT

THE MOMENT TO SHOUT

God's Way to Face Walls

LUIS PALAU

MULTNOMAH PRESS
PORTLAND, OREGON 97266

Verses marked **TLB** taken from *The Living Bible*, copyright 1971 by Tyndale House Publishers, Wheaton, Illinois. Used by permission.

Verses marked **KJV** taken from the King James Version of the Bible.

All other verses taken from the *Revised Standard Version* of the Bible, copyright 1946, 1952, © 1971, 1973. Division of Christian Education, National Council of the Churches of Christ in the USA. Used by permission.

Published by Multnomah Press
Portland, Oregon 97266
Printed in the United States of America

Second Printing 1981

The Library of Congress has provided the following CIP data for the trade paperback edition:
Palau, Luis, 1934–
    The moment to shout/ Luis Palau; foreword by Ray Stedman. — Portland, Or.: Multnomah Press, c1977.
    160 p.; 21 cm.
    ISBN 0-930014-16-2 : $3.95

    1. Christian life—1960-   2. Bible. O.T. Joshua—Meditations.   I. Title.
BV4501.2.P267   170'.202   77-4593
                                MARC

Library of Congress   78

ISBN 0-930014-84-7

This book is dedicated to Dr. Ray C. Stedman, whose teaching and life example taught me these truths, and to my wife, Patricia, who helps me live them out.

Luis Palau

Table of Contents

Foreword

Scripture charges both pastor *and* evangelist with the necessity of "equipping the saints to do the work of the ministry" (Ephesians 4:12). But, it is extremely rare to find an evangelist who takes that charge seriously. Most are so busy with soul winning that they give little concern to building up their converts with solid Bible study.

Luis Palau is that rare evangelist. He is not only at home on the platform but is equally proficient with the pen, and is a capable Bible teacher with a deep concern for the maturing of his converts.

His previous volume on the life of the Apostle Peter, his volume on Jacob and Joseph, *The Schemer and the Dreamer*, and this present study in Joshua reveal his ability to make Bible truth live. The pictures of the spiritual pilgrimage of a believer depicted in the book of Joshua are delightfully unfolded in this popular study. It should prove to be a great help to new believers of all ages who are themselves crossing the wilderness from the bondage of Egypt to the liberty of Canaan.

As one who has followed his developing ministry for many years, I welcome this additional study from the pen of Luis Palau.

Dr. Ray C. Stedman

Introduction

When the people of Israel crossed the Red Sea, they shouted a song of Moses, a song of thanksgiving. Slavery was behind them. Taskmasters were behind them. All the cruelty of Egypt—the house of bondage—was behind them. They shouted for joy.

But in a few short weeks they were weeping, complaining against Moses and complaining against the God who had just delivered them. So the Lord caused them to wander aimlessly in the desert.

Is this your spiritual situation? It was mine for eight long dry years.

I was converted to Christ when I was 12 at a camp in Argentina, South America. To let everyone know of my decision, I bought a Bible, carried it under my arm, and told every friend I had about the Lord Jesus. What a happy year! Some of my fellow students made fun of me, but I was so happy in Christ that I even enjoyed the mocking.

However, after about a year and a half, I began to cool down. One day I lost my Bible on a streetcar and I didn't even bother to buy another. As the days went by, I left all my desire to witness behind me and all my joy, too.

Four or five years went by before I even took one

little step back in returning toward the Lord. What wasted years! Then it took another eight years to actually come into the fulness of Jesus Christ. When I did, I was twenty-four years old instead of twelve. The streetcar had rolled a long way toward the end of the line.

Many of us have gone through that. It's almost a certain thing that each one of us will go through "a desert experience" after accepting Christ. We lose that first flush of triumph, that first song of joy —that inner something that seemed to radiate from within.

In Revelation 2, Jesus Christ tells the church of Ephesus, "You have left your first love." That first love is a new awareness of sins forgiven—a new sense of His indwelling presence and love that so fills a new believer with joy and zeal that you can't keep him silent. He has to tell everyone. Many older Christians step back, fold their arms, and smile a knowing smile, thinking, "I wonder how soon this will fade out?"

It doesn't have to fade out at all! It is possible to go on *forever* in this first love as a victorious Christian, but most of us do not. Instead, we waste precious years in the desert of unbelief and somewhere in the sandy wastes we lose our first love. One day we look in the canteen and it's dry. We become frantic and desperate. A wild, frightening dryness grips us. "This is the end," we say.

Or is it? Perhaps it could be a new beginning. . . .

You might be nearer than you ever dreamed to the moment to shout!

1

Joshua and
the Second Rest

Can you imagine what the children of Israel felt before the Egyptian army vanished under the Red Sea?

Pharaoh and the boys had their chariots in high gear, coming straight for them.

"We've had it now," the people said. "There's no way out!"

They turned on Moses. "Look what you got us into! What did you have in mind, bringing us out here? Target practice for the Egyptians?"

But then the Lord opened up the Red Sea and the Israelites scrambled across on dry ground. Smoking on their heels, Pharaoh's crack storm-troopers tried the same trick but found the road closed—right over their heads.

As the mighty east wind faded to an ocean breeze and waves returned to their ancient ebb and flow, you could hear the audible sigh from two and a half million Israelites. They were experiencing what we will call *the first rest*.

"Hey! We're free from Egypt! Really free, can you believe it? We made it through the sea and—praise God—what a relief!"

But it wasn't really the complete rest they were

looking for. They wandered for another forty years until their bones bleached in the Sinai sun. Free from Egypt? No doubt about it. But freed for what?

During those long wilderness years the children of Israel were ever conscious that something was missing. They had found the first rest, but they longed for another. Finally, it was the children of that first generation who entered into *the second rest*, the rest of being in the place where God intended them to be.

The Old Testament book of Joshua takes up the narrative right here with the people who crossed over the Jordan onto victory soil. Illustrated in Joshua are the principles of spiritual rest and the spiritual victory that produces true rest in the Christian life.

Why plunge into a study of Joshua? To me, it is the guidebook to victory. With the Holy Spirit's help, we will approach it as a picture—an illustration of your walk with Jesus Christ. Contained in the pages of this dynamic Old Testament book are truths with explosive implications for New Testament believers. Are you living the filled-to-the-brim sort of life that God intended for you?

There are two rests for the believer as he receives Christ as his Savior and senses a surge of relief. He realizes that all of his sins—every ugly one of them —are now completely forgiven. Here is a great rest of conscience, to feel washed, cleansed, and purified. All things are new.

But it isn't enough. After a few weeks or months he feels restless again. He knows he's forgiven. He knows he's a child of God. In his heart he knows he's going to heaven if he should die. But something's missing. Deep in his inner parts there is a restless longing, a wistful sense of something half finished with the better part to come. It may be years before he experiences the second rest.

If we allow the indwelling Lord Jesus Christ to control us, we're going to have rest of heart, mind, and spirit. For He said, "Come to me, all who labor and are heavy laden, and I will give you rest."

That's the rest of forgiveness—the first rest, purchased with the blood of God's sinless Son. There follows the second rest in the next verse.

"Take my yoke upon you, and learn from me; for I am gentle and lowly in heart, and you will find rest for your souls."

There are two rests in this passage, and there are two rests for the people of God.

Jesus Christ has come to *indwell* us. Not until He begins to *control* us, however, will we find the rest that every Christian heart is looking for—the rest that eluded me for so many years.

Call it what you will. Argue all you please. But allow this one fact: Across the country and around the world by the hundreds of thousands, Christians are clamoring for daily reality in their walk with God. Believing in a risen, living Lord, they catch glimpses from the Bible of what their life in Christ could really be. And they want it!

"But how? How?"

Unfortunately, many never get the right teaching. In no time, they go right back to their old ways. They fall right back into the old pattern of living for self, never learning how to live in the land that God

15

has promised—how to live on victory soil.

But there is a way. God never intended his people to live in defeat. So why wait in the wilderness? Cross over with Joshua into all God longs for you to be. Step by step, take possession of everything your Heavenly Father intends for you to thoroughly live out and enjoy.

In Joshua we see a picture of that Spirit-filled life.

> *"Moses my servant is dead; now therefore arise, go over this Jordan, you and all this people, into the land which I am giving to them, to the people of Israel" (Joshua 1:2).*

Notice that this life is the free gift of God. We cannot attain it by the strength of our self-effort; we cannot obtain it through the struggle of our striving. Sometimes we feel as though God has an angel assigned to each one of us with a clip-board and a tally-sheet. When we get enough "good marks" he says, "Okay. Great job. That was good work, Number 757. You're qualified for promotion now, so step on in to the Spirit-filled life."

It could never happen that way! If we had a thousand lifetimes, we could never earn enough "good marks." Rest, victory, satisfaction—the people of Israel were given these things by their gracious God. And so are we.

The second thing we notice is that even though the land was given, it had to be possessed.

> *"Every place that the sole of your foot will tread upon I have given to you, as I promised to Moses" (Joshua 1:3).*

Wherever they set their foot down, the land was theirs. Although they had the title deed from God, they could never really enjoy the land until they actually went in through the gates and took over.

It's the same way in our spiritual life. Everyone who has received Jesus Christ as Savior has the all-powerful Son of the living God camped in his innermost being. Every Christian has title deed to a life that overflows its banks, brimming with the presence and power of God Himself.

> *For in him (Christ) the whole fulness of deity dwells bodily, and you have come to fulness of life in him, who is the head of all rule and authority (Colossians 2:9-10).*

So many believers are ignorant of this great truth. Instead of marching in to possess all that belongs to them in the Lord, they are content to hang the title deed on their wall and remain in the wilderness. They haven't appropriated everything that Jesus Christ intended them to grasp. Struggling and battling in their own strength to be conquering Christians, they find their fervent activity only sinks them deeper in the mire.

They weep, pray, beg, and buy tickets to every Christian life seminar that comes to town. They read, they seek counsel, they turn over new leaves like an elm in the springtime—but never quite make it. Somehow, even though the life they crave belongs to them, they've never really claimed it. They haven't set their foot down. They haven't possessed what God has already given them.

Third, notice that this was also an abundant life.

"From the wilderness and this Lebanon as far as the great river, the river Euphrates, all the land of the Hittites to the Great Sea toward the going down of the sun shall be your territory" (Joshua 1:4).

The Lord speaks of the land as flowing with milk and honey. It's a lovely, radiant picture, *flowing* with milk and honey. It is a pleasing land, where the blessing of God sings in the little brooks and sighs in the moonlit forests. It is a productive land, rich in nourishing produce and boundless pastures.

Yet, instead of going in to possess all this bounty, the Israelites track about in the desert, perhaps even convincing themselves, "This must be Canaan." Camping on the sand and rock, they tell themselves that it's grass. After a while they assume there is nothing more to look forward to in life.

Isn't this true of our lives as well? We who have received the Lord Jesus as Savior have enough and more than we could ever need to satisfy us. In Christ we have a great, continual banquet providing for constant spiritual energy and fresh-daily spiritual strength. What a delicious experience to know Jesus Christ!

Tragically, many Christians never find it this way. Too many drag along on a crackers-and-water diet with never enough stamina to get them through the day. They want to be faithful, they pray to be faithful, they beg God to make them faithful, but they rarely ever enjoy the milk and honey. They have not yet tasted the second rest.

Verse 5 assures us that there will be conflict in this good land, but only to demonstrate God's certain victory on behalf of His trusting children.

> *"No man shall be able to stand before you all the days of your life; as I was with Moses, so I will be with you; I will not fail you or forsake you" (Joshua 1:5).*

God never promises an absence of conflict. But in that conflict He promises something that makes life's skirmishes infinitely worthwhile . . . Himself.

> *"I will be with you; I will not fail you or forsake you."*

WE CAN OVERCOME

This last year in Mexico, my family, myself, and the whole Team faced an unrelenting torrent of conflict, things that we never remotely anticipated. As Ephesians 6 puts it, the "fiery darts" came from directions for which we were totally unprepared. People that we thought were so mature would approach us and say unbelievable things and unconsciously serve as Satan's instruments to discourage us.

Once again, the Holy Spirit had to remind me, "Luis, when did I ever promise that you would be free from trouble in this world?" An old verse that my mom taught me when I was a little boy came back to me this year with fresh clarity:

> *"In the world you have tribulation; but be of*

good cheer, I have overcome the world" (John 16:33b).

Before I understood that Christ actually lives within me because I'm a Christian, I used to look at that verse and say, "Yes, Lord, You've overcome the world. But then, You are You and I am me. You are there and I am here. You have overcome the world, but I am certainly *not* overcoming the world. Where are You when I need you?"

This was a twisted attitude, but it was there nevertheless. But then, years later, I coupled the words, "I have overcome the world," with the thought, "I live in you." Ah, that makes all the difference, doesn't it?

So the Lord Jesus Christ has overcome the world. How does that help me? Just that He happens to be living inside me. That repaints the whole scene. I will have tribulation—yes. But the living Christ indwells me; and because He has overcome the world, if I permit Him to do so, He will overcome it once again—*through* me. Filling me with His limitless power and wisdom, the King of Kings continues to conquer and reign in me.

> *If, because of one man's trespass, death reigned through that one man, much more will those who receive the abundance of grace and the free gift of righteousness reign in life through the one man Jesus Christ (Romans 5:17).*

Being filled with God's Spirit was never intended to be a ticket to trouble-free days and ceaseless sunshine.

Fourth, in verses 6-9, we have the secret of it all. Shake together all the programs, prescriptions, and panaceas for success in the Christian life and this is what rolls out every time: Simple obedience—that is, acting upon God's clear word of direction.

> *"Be strong and of good courage; for you shall cause this people to inherit the land which I swore to their fathers to give them.*

> *"Only be strong and very courageous, being careful to do according to all the law which Moses my servant commanded you; turn not from it to the right hand or to the left, that you may have good success wherever you go.*

> *"This book of the law shall not depart out of your mouth, but you shall meditate on it day and night, that you may be careful to do according to all that is written in it; for then you shall make your way prosperous, and then you shall have good success.*

> *"Have I not commanded you? Be strong and of good courage; be not frightened, neither be dismayed; for the LORD your God is with you wherever you go"* (Joshua 1:6-9).

OUR HEARTS MELTED WITHIN US

In chapter two we have the remarkable story of Rahab. This woman was of a very low, sad life—a harlot. We won't try to discover why God chose a woman of this caliber to fulfill His purpose, but He did.

Would you have chosen her? I wouldn't have. I probably would have taken her aside and said in a low voice, "Now, why don't you help us by passing out handbills or some tracts. On the other side of town. I don't think we can have you appear on the crusade platform. Just pass out some tracts or go make some lemonade in the kitchen."

Honestly now, we would have never considered picking out a prostitute for a major role of ministry, would we? But the Lord did. More than that, He recorded her name in His eternal Word and singled her out for special recognition in the New Testament's Hall of Faith in Hebrews 11. It's quite an amazing thing, how God works. He always does things differently and that's the delightful thing about walking with the Lord. He breaks all the rules we set up. He does it His way in His time and He works by His own rules. That's what makes the Christian life exciting.

But here is something startling. When the two Israelite spies came into Rahab's apartment, she told them:

> *"We have heard how the LORD dried up the water of the Red Sea before you when you came out of Egypt, and what you did to the two kings of the Amorites that were beyond the Jordan, to Sihon and Og, whom you utterly destroyed.*
>
> *"And as soon as we heard it, our hearts melted, and there was no courage left in any man, because of you; for the LORD your God is he who is God in heaven above and on earth beneath"* (Joshua 2:10-11).

Do you remember what the ten spies had reported to Moses? "We can't take control over these people," they said. "They are strong. They are giants. They live in fortified cities. And what are we? Just a bunch of grasshoppers!" (Numbers 13:17-33).

So for forty years the Israelites had been running away, taking endless laps in a desolate desert. No one dared go near the Promised Land because, in their distrust of God's promise and in disobedience to His command, they had become afraid of its inhabitants. And now they find that during the same forty years the people of Jericho had been just as terrified of them!

Every morning the citizens of Jericho woke up with the dread that the terrible Israelites were going to march in and take over. Somehow, the fear of God had overtaken them and they were absolutely trembling behind their mighty walls. And to think that the children of Israel wandered and withered and wasted their lives in the wilderness, never once setting foot on the glorious land of promise, because they refused to believe God. The land could have been theirs in short order; but, instead, they suffered in their own rebellion.

Is this your spiritual situation? It could be. It was mine for eight years. It is the sad story of thousands.

I remember a minister in a Central American country. He was one of the most bitter ministers of the gospel I've ever met. He was also a good friend of mine. He hates Americans, hates his fellow countrymen, and can't stand missionaries. He's against the imperialists, the communists, and Rockefeller. He's against everything.

One day we were standing together at a bus stop, waiting for a bus that would take me to the little church where I was to preach. I said, "Juan, what have you been preaching on lately?"

"I'm preaching on the victorious Christian life."

"I see. Where did you get your outline? What are you using?"

"Oh, I picked up one of the books by Moody Press. Great outlines, just great. We're having a great time."

Later, I said, "Juan, what are you preaching about when you talk about the victorious Christian life?"

He gave me some of the outlines.

I said, "You know something, Juan? You can preach all you want to on being a victorious Christian, but your whole life preaches something different."

"What do you mean, Luis?"

"My friend, you are bitter against the missionaries, bitter against your fellow pastors, and bitter against businessmen. It oozes from your pores; it colors every word that you say. I've never heard one good word from you about anyone. How can you preach victorious Christianity?"

"You're right, Luis, I'm going to quit preaching that until I really experience it."

I don't think he's come into it yet. I was there recently and didn't get to see him, but they told me he's the same old "dad." Never changed. What a pity.

You can talk about it. I certainly did. I have some outlines from the old days—beautiful outlines—but I was living a completely defeated life. There are many people living this way. Their Christianity looks great on paper—every "T" crossed and "I" dotted—but their lives say something else.

Rahab might never have been invited to sit on the platform at an evangelistic crusade or even to take part in the ladies' missionary circle, but in God's eyes her faith was something beautiful. For this reason she was chosen of God to be saved out of the destruction falling on Jericho. Though a pagan, she also came through faith to enjoy the land of milk and honey. In contrast, a whole generation of "God's people" who came out of Egypt never, never enjoyed the land or their life with God. Isn't that sad? They fell because of unbelief in the wasteland. Redeemed from bondage, they were out of Egypt. But they never got in to enjoy the fruits of redemption and victory in the Promised Land.

There are thousands of evangelical Christians in this same situation. I've met them all over the world—good people. They are fundamental in their doctrine. They love the Word of God and appreciate hearing good, solid, Biblical exposition. They really mean everything they say and would be willing to fight to the end in defense of the truth. After all, they are truly redeemed by the blood of the Lamb. All of that is good and praiseworthy—*yet they never, never truly enjoy their life in Christ.*

Some will argue, "Who said the Christian life was to be enjoyed? We are only 'strangers and pilgrims,'

25

the joy is 'over there.' " That was the conclusion I came to about ten years ago. I came to the U.S. from Argentina. Down in South America my friends and I had a daily radio program, tent campaigns, and evangelistic meetings in towns, villages, and across the countryside. But for all of this, my life was lived in personal defeat.

It wasn't that I was living in some deep immorality; I was simply defeated. My tongue was bitter. Criticism, envy, and personal problems simmered inside of me and sometimes boiled over. Yet I loved Jesus Christ and wanted to serve Him.

Then, ten years ago in the United States, God finally helped me to realize the difference between trying to live by my own efforts and learning to live in the indwelling power of Jesus Christ. Only eternity (and maybe my wife) will be able to describe the difference this made in me.

There are many who would say (when they see someone who is always just a little too happy in Christ), "I don't know about Joe. Every time I meet him, he seems to be happy. Every time I shake his hand, he seems excited. Every time you talk to him, he's got problems; but he says, 'The Lord helped me.' I just don't trust anyone who's *that* happy."

For so long we've observed the "abnormal" that when someone comes by radiating real Christian joy and peace, we think *they* need counseling!

"Hey, this person is on some kind of 'high.' We need to bring him down to reality. He can't be going around with that positive attitude and bubbling spirit all the time. He can't be for real, can he?"

Driving to the office a few weeks ago, I heard

someone on the radio speaking on a Scripture passage that we've all heard many times:

> But the fruit of the Spirit is love, joy, peace, patience, kindness, goodness, faithfulness, gentleness, self-control; against such there is no law (Galatians 5:22-23).

I was waiting at a red light and the radio preacher said something that almost made me miss the green one.

"Do you know what that means—'against such there is no law'?" he asked. "It means that there is no law against loving too much. God will never come alongside of you and say, 'You've loved enough, better put on the brakes awhile.' There is no law against love."

Then he said, "There is no law against too much joy. You can never be too joyful in Jesus Christ. God is never going to say, 'You've had enough fun for awhile. Now I'm going to cool it for you.' "

The Lord says, "Rejoice always." It is we Christians who too often would like to sour up people. If we see them too happy, we say they are "superficial." But not the Lord. He says, "There is no law against joy." You can have as much of it as you want if you allow the indwelling Christ to control you. You can have it all the time; it doesn't have to stop.

There's no law against too much peace that says, "You've been peaceful enough for the last three weeks, now worry a little bit." Sometimes we're almost afraid to enjoy the peace of Christ for fear that something will come crashing in and shatter it like a thin pane of glass. But the peace of Christ is not made of the same fragile material as the world's peace. The peace He gives can weather any crisis and withstand any circumstance.

> *"Peace I leave with you; my peace I give to you; not as the world gives do I give to you. Let not your hearts be troubled, neither let them be afraid" (John 14:27).*

Don't let unbelief deny you of your spiritual birthright in Christ. The land of God's profound promises belongs to every born-again Christian, not just to certain "special people." It belongs to you.

How long has it been since you've taken your title deed down off the wall and really gripped its provisions?

1. Control over the Law of Sin
For the law of the Spirit of life in Christ Jesus has set me free from the law of sin and death (Romans 8:2).

2. The Sense of Nearness to Our Father and the Experience of His Guidance
For all who are led by the Spirit of God are sons of God. For you did not receive the spirit of slavery to fall back into fear, but you have received the spirit of sonship. When we cry, "Abba! Father!" it is the Spirit himself bearing witness with our spirit that we are children of God (Romans 8:14-16).

3. All the Experiences of Life under His Sovereign Control
We know that in everything God works for good with those who love him, who are called according to his

purpose (Romans 8:28).

4. Victory over Circumstances
No, in all these things we are more than conquerors through him who loved us (Romans 8:37).

5. Peace in the Inner Person, the Spirit
And let the peace of Christ rule in your hearts, to which indeed you were called in the one body. And be thankful (Colossians 3:15).

6. Self-Control
For God did not give us a spirit of timidity but a spirit of power and love and self-control (2 Timothy 1:7).

Stop a moment. Are these words living realities in your experience or are they merely words on a page? Whatever your answer, come with me one step further into this land of victory—the place of second rest.

2

Everything He Is
for Everything I Face

Our team has an office in a tri-county city. Portland, Oregon, sits on a point where three of the state's counties merge and there is a portion of Portland in each of them.

This book of Joshua is "tri-county" also. We find references to three basic territories—three types of land. Where the authority of one territory ends, the authority of another territory begins.

In Portland, you may find yourself bouncing along at night on a bumpy, winding road in the West Hills until you hit the county line—and everything changes! Suddenly the inky darkness is flooded by street lights lining a road that has become smooth and level. Crossing into the area of a different territorial authority—the highway changes.

As the book of Joshua begins, the Israelites have left behind the authority of the first territory and its governor and are preparing to enter into the third territory after wandering in the second one for forty years.

SLAVE TERRITORY

Ruled by a cruel, tyrannical king who thought of himself as almighty—almost a god—the first land was an ungracious host to the people of Israel. Enslaved, driven, beaten, and despised, the Israelites were treated little better than cattle to suit the purposes of this dictator—Pharaoh.

The God that the Israelites were trying to serve was the God whom the king mocked and detested. Overall, the first territory was one of chains and poverty and tears—not to mention the sting of the whip. Pharaoh originated two practices which would haunt these Hebrew people for centuries to come: the shame of being huddled and herded by hardened enemy soldiers, and the humiliation of having their national pride viciously smashed by a government enflamed with hate. This was Egypt.

We were all born in Egypt (and I don't mean the Cairo General Hospital). All of us were born in the first territory under the territorial authority of Satan as slaves of a tyrant who hates us and hates our God. We were all born "children of wrath."

> *Among these we all once lived in the passions of our flesh, following the desires of body and mind, and so we were by nature children of wrath, like the rest of mankind (Ephesians 2:3).*

WILDERNESS TERRITORY

The second territory was outside Egypt, a land of frustration and wandering. Zig-zagging back and forth in this arid waste, the children of Israel were never quite satisfied, never quite able to rid themselves of hunger. It was better than Egypt, but not nearly satisfying. In fact, not much better at all! Pharaoh was gone, the chains were gone, the whip was gone, but everybody felt restless—there had to be something better ahead.

It was the "country" of defeat and discouragement as the road looped endlessly and never led anywhere. It was the place of knowing that one is in the wrong place at the wrong time. It was a land of quarrelling and murmuring, where no one seemed happy, neither the leader nor the people. It was the land of doing right in one's own eyes, not in God's eyes. That was the desert.

This speaks to us of where so many Christians are living for too many years of their lives. They're out of Egypt. Oh yes! They're not under Satanic control any more. They're not slaves of Satan or driven by him, as non-Christians are. But still, they're wandering and restless—unsatisfied. They have replaced lord-Satan with lord-Self and have still not found the true Lord. Self can be the most tyrannical master of all, and escaping from slavery of one sort into slavery of another sort is hardly the solution for which our spirits have longed.

HOME TERRITORY

Finally, there is the Land of Rest. This "shall be your territory" (Joshua 1:4). This is the territory where God wants us to live, not in the chains of Satan, not wandering in a cheerless desert with its dryness and hunger and thirst. *This* is our territory.

This is where we belong—*this* is the land of promise. We belong where God wants us to live. Are you in that place right now?

What is this Home Territory like? We were told the land is given to us.

> *"Moses my servant is dead; now therefore arise, go over this Jordan, you and all this people, into the land which I am giving to them, to the people of Israel" (Joshua 1:2).*

God's ideal plan for every Christian man and every Christian woman is that each live a life that is satisfying, hopeful, productive, and triumphant. This is God's "county." Are you living on the right side of the county line?

In your experience, do you find that life is charged with meaning in Jesus Christ? Is your daily walk characterized by victory over sin? Or are you wandering, dissatisfied, confused?

There is one point I find that I can never stress enough. It is simply this: A victorious Christian life is something that God *gives* to us. Wherever I've traveled, all over the world, I find Christians who are still trying to "earn" the winning, Spirit-filled life they long to possess. They feel that there is something *they* must do to have a life that brings glory to their God. This is absolutely untrue. Like Paul, we may strain every nerve and press toward the mark, but finally we must realize that "God is at work in you, both to will and to work for his good pleasure" (Philippians 2:13).

34

OLD MAN—NEW MAN

When a person is born, he is born an "old man." What is the "old man," the man outside of Christ? We hesitate to voice it, don't we? The more you study the Bible, the more you realize that a person not "in Christ" is a person controlled by the spirit of this world—Satan, the Enemy.

And you he made alive, when you were dead through the trespasses and sins in which you once walked, following the course of this world, following the prince of the power of the air, the spirit that is now at work in the sons of disobedience (Ephesians 2:1-2).

The three parts of man—the human spirit, the human soul, and even the human body were designed to contain God (1 Corinthians 6:15, 19). We were made to be indwelt by a Person. And that Person is God.

When God created Adam and Eve, they were created to be filled and controlled by Him. Yet our father and mother rejected that plan and listened instead to the Enemy.

Expelled from the Garden of Eden, they were controlled by Satan from the moment they rebelled. From that time on, each one of us has been born in sin, the Bible tells us. Each is born, not with God controlling us or indwelling us, but alienated from the life of the God who loves us.

Until God confronts us with Jesus Christ, and by the Spirit convicts us of our sin, makes us repent, and moves us to trust Christ, we are all children of wrath. The nice little boys and girls, that fine-looking neighbor, that cultured and educated M.D. down the street—without Jesus Christ all are as much children of wrath controlled by Satan as a drunk on a downtown street.

This is a hard truth. We don't like to accept this fact, do we? Jesus Christ said to those who questioned Him, "You are of your father the devil." Doesn't that make your flesh crawl? I've been told, "Hey, tread easy on that—don't preach on that." It seems so harsh to say to a group of people who refuse to believe on the Lord Jesus or who simply ignore Him, "You know that you are of your father, the devil." It's one of the most insulting things you can say to them.

Why is it insulting? Because no human being was designed to be controlled by Satan. God did not intend humans to be sons of the devil. Yet, that's the way it is until Jesus Christ gathers the reins in a life. We have to face it.

We don't like to admit that there is nothing good in ourselves. Paul said, "For I know that nothing good dwells within me, that is, in my flesh" (Romans 7:18a). We're prone to say, "Well, there's a little bit of good and a little bit of bad. It's true that sometimes I'm not as nice as I should be. Okay, so I'm a little nasty to the old lady once in awhile. And . . . I do get a little unbearable from time to time. But on the other hand, I'm pretty lovable, too. I'm not that bad!"

Francis Schaeffer was right, of course, when he said: "Man is great—but lost."

The Bible says that a person outside of Jesus

Christ *is all bad*. All his donations to charity are nothing in God's sight. In terms of a right standing before a holy God, all his efforts at "being good" are simply not good enough. They are in fact *no good* in God's estimation—a waste of time.

But "if any one is in Christ, he is a new creation; the old has passed away, behold, the new has come" (2 Corinthians 5:17). When in space and time a child of wrath clasps his hands in the outstretched hands of God's Son, at that moment he becomes a new person. The old spirit, the old indweller— Satan—is evicted. The one who used to control this person's thinking, emotions, and will is forced *out* and Jesus Christ comes *in* to dwell in that human spirit.

OUT OF EGYPT—INTO THE DESERT

". . . He who is united to the Lord becomes one spirit with him" (1 Corinthians 6:17). Jesus Christ comes in, takes up residence within me, and I become a new man in Him. At that moment, when He enters my life, I leave Egypt behind me and enter the desert. I am en route to the home territory.

Not understanding what has really happened to me, I may begin to wander for awhile. Most people, when they receive Christ, don't realize what has happened to them. Someone has told them, "Look, Jesus Christ loves you. He died for you, He wants to forgive your sins and give you a new life. Will you believe?" They feel a sense of restlessness, that something isn't right, and they say, "Yes, I believe."

Some of us received Christ when a counselor said to us, "Look, you are such a sinner that unless you receive Christ, you are going to hell." That's what a man told me. I was twelve, attending a youth camp. He led me out of my tent and said, "Luis, do you believe that you're a sinner?"

I said, "Yes, I do." I knew it, not only because they taught me the Bible, but because I was a filthy little sinner, even though I was only twelve.

He said, "You know what God has to do with sinners?"

I said, "Yes, He's got to punish them."

"Do you know how you can be saved from being condemned for your sins? What do you have to do?" he asked.

I answered, "Believe on the Lord Jesus Christ and thou shalt be saved."

The counselor asked then, "Luis, have you believed on the Lord Jesus Christ? Have you put your trust in Him?"

I replied, "No."

"Wouldn't you like to do it now and be sure?" he asked.

So we bowed our heads and he led me to receive Jesus Christ as my Savior. I became a child of God and I knew it (John 1:12). But do you think I really understood *everything* that had happened to me? All I knew, and it made me terrifically happy, was that I wasn't going to go to hell when I died. That was the greatest feeling.

But it took me many more years to actually understand what had happened at the campground. I was safely out of Egypt. I was in the desert, but I really didn't understand what it was to mean in my everyday experience.

Years went by and my footprints mingled in the desert sands with the footprints of thousands of other dissatisfied, quarreling, unfulfilled Christians. There were times when the desert seemed to blossom but most of the time it just felt like empty wilderness. Driven on and on by spiritual hunger and thirst, I came at last to the fords of the Jordan and the territory of promise across the way.

Back in that camp, when I was a young boy, a counselor named Frank Chandler was God's instrument to lead me out of slave territory into a liberating union with the Son of God. All along the desert way, God brought others across my path to help bring me out of that parched place into the new territory. Finally, I understood and crossed over with a song.

When a person first receives Christ, he is usually very ignorant of what happened. Unless the Holy Spirit of God begins to teach him through the Scripture and you and I become available to the Lord to counsel this new person, he may lose many choice years in the desert, never discovering the magnificent heritage that is his in Christ.

It needn't happen this way. No child of God need ever waste months and years outside "the promised land"—the promised life. If we are pliable, teachable, tender to His voice, and resting on His promises, it is His delight that we should march straight out of slavery and into a life of victory. The principle in Joshua of "the desert" corresponds to the New Testament teaching on "walking in the flesh," carnality. It is the earnest longing of the Holy Spirit that God's beloved children leave the carnal life behind and enjoy the fulness of His fellowship and great depths of His love.

WHAT'S A VESSEL FOR?

Human beings were created to be indwelt. Many passages in the New Testment mention this.

> We have this treasure in earthen vessels, to show that the transcendent power belongs to God and not to us (2 Corinthians 4:7).

What's a vessel for? It is designed to contain something. A drink of water, a bouquet of daisies, a collection of pennies—something is inside.

We are meant to be containers. When we invited the Lord Jesus to enter our lives, He actually filled our being with Himself and will stay there forever. We were created to be containers of Christ. The rest of our Christian life is spent not only learning what it means to have Christ indwelling us but learning how to allow the indwelling Christ to so control us, mold us, and remake us that we become vessels that honor God, "conformed to the image of His Son" (Romans 8:29).

Earthen vessels—clay jars? Certainly. Not very lovely in ourselves, but containing none other than the Lord of the universe. Therefore, we become "vessels unto honor." This is something over which we have no control. This is what Christ did for us before we could do anything for Christ. He came into our lives when we didn't understand what it was all about. He made us His vessels.

This is something that God does out of sheer grace, out of love. He came to live in your heart because *He chose* to. Actually, all you can do is say, "Thank You, Lord. I don't understand why on earth You would want to come into my life; but I worship and praise You, Lord, that one day, when I didn't know anything about You, except perhaps a little intellectually, You chose to take up residence in me. Thank You.

"Now that I understand that You are alive in me, I want to begin to experience Your very life, controlling and empowering me to please God and bring honor to Him."

You and I didn't choose to be converted to God. God chose us to be saved, and we responded to His call, by faith. Who began the good work? God began it. Who will bring it to completion? He will. ". . . He who began a good work in you will bring it to completion at the day of Jesus Christ" (Philippians 1:6). He began the good work within us when we accepted Christ. Now He is working in us.

The sooner we submit by faith to what He's trying to do in our hearts and lives, the sooner we'll be molded into His image. If we resist the moving and molding of His Spirit within us, He's going to corner us, allow us to run into a wall, bang our heads, go through troubles and all the weird situations that we bring upon ourselves.

The Lord is not going to force Himself on us. He will rather simply let us futilely thrash about until we finally drop on the floor, saying, "Lord, what's going on?" Then the Lord can do His good work in us once again.

We've established that the victorious life is something that is given to us. We don't work for it; it's a free gift. It's ours, but we must move out and take hold of it. Actually make it ours.

Suppose *Reader's Digest* called you and said, "Congratulations. You are the grand prize winner of $50,000 and we are depositing this sum of money in a bank account under your name. It's all yours whenever you want it."

Think of it! $50,000, sitting there—all yours. But, actually, you don't enjoy it or get any use from it until you go and draw on it.

It's exactly the same with the indwelling Jesus Christ. "We have this treasure in earthen vessels." There it is, the treasure. Jesus Christ in all His fulness, closer than hands or feet, closer than breathing. What we must learn is how to draw upon all that He is and all that He has for us.

This is why it's a mistake to pray, "Oh, Lord, enter my life. Lord, give me more of this, make me more of that." Christ already indwells us. He's all there. We can't have any more than that. Remember that word, "You have come to fulness of life in him" (Colossians 2:10).

The point is, how much does Christ have of you? We have all of Christ that there is to have. Even when we grow and mature in the Christian life, we're not going to have more of Christ. He will have more of us.

He's there! The $50,000 is all ours and it's all there. How much we enjoy the $50,000 depends on how much we draw from the bank and actually begin to use.

The Lord came into my life when I was twelve years old and he's been the same Lord Jesus Christ ever since. But for years I didn't understand what I had. It's not that when I was twenty-four, somehow the Lord Jesus acquired more power or greater fulness. He was the same Lord. It's just that I understood more, and I began to allow Him to do what He's always wanted to do in me.

> *I am crucified with Christ: nevertheless I live; yet not I, but Christ liveth in me: and the life which I now live in the flesh I live by the faith of the Son of God, who loved me, and gave himself for me (Galatians 2:20 KJV).*

I have been crucified with Christ. What does that mean? It means that on the day I was converted, the old spirit left. The old man died on the day I received Christ. *I* was crucified with Christ then, and *I* am *still* crucified with Christ.

The cross was the end of the dominion of Satan over my life. The day that Christ came into my heart, Satan went out. *I* was crucified right then and there. Crucifixion means death.

The old person who indwelt me (Satan) left. Nevertheless, I live. I'm alive. But it's not I that am alive; it is Christ who dwells in me. This is something we must understand if we're going to truly enjoy the Christian life. Satan will never again take over in our lives. "For sin will have no dominion over you, since you are not under law but under grace" (Romans 6:14). It is not that I will never commit sin again. Yes, sadly, I still do. But the old enslaver is

43

gone. Gone forever! Jesus Christ fills all my spirit.

But Lord, I'm So Weak!

> *. . . it is no longer I who live, but Christ who lives in me; and the life I now live in the flesh I live by faith in the Son of God, who loved me and gave himself for me (Galatians 2:20b).*

Now my life is controlled, not by the old spirit, but by the new Spirit, the Spirit of the Lord Jesus Christ. "The life I now live in the flesh, I live by faith." I am trusting Him every moment of every day in all my circumstances, my problems, my temptations. He's here. He's been indwelling me since I was twelve.

How long has He been living in *your* life—one year, fifteen, thirty, forty? All right, He's there. The question is, how much is He controlling your daily walk?

We must take possession of what is already ours. When temptation comes, we must learn to face it in the empowering Christ. When opportunities to witness come, it will not be in our own strength that we step through the open door. When an opportunity for service comes, we do not face the task alone. It is the indwelling Christ who will perform these works through me. This is not an easy concept to grasp and by nature we don't like it. Too often we rebel against it because our minds are conditioned by the thinking of the world. We proudly say, "I can do it, if I put my mind to it." Well, why not try? Try to overcome temptation in your own power. Try to serve God in your own power. You'll soon fall flat on your face, defeated and miserable, like thousands of other Christians.

They're trying to live the Christian life in their own strength. We were never designed to serve God in our own strength. We were made to serve God in the strength of the indwelling Jesus Christ.

"I can do all things in him who strengthens me" (Philippians 4:13). Where is Christ when I need Him to strengthen me? Do I have to call for Him every time I need Him? Many of us have the idea that the Lord saved us, made us children of God, and then He let us loose in the world to fend for ourselves. When we need Him, we can call on Him; and, if He's listening and if we're "staying in touch" with Him, He might come to our rescue. If not, we must continue fending for ourselves.

MONDAY MORNING AGAIN!

How many people start the day off with a wail instead of a confident prayer? Instead of praising God for what He's going to do, they say, "Oh, Lord, here's Monday morning. It was so good yesterday. The church service was tremendous, but here we go again into the nitty-gritty of daily life. Lord, you know how weak I am when I get around some of those non-Christians. Please help me, Lord, to do the right thing today.

"Lord, you know when they tell some dirty joke, how it kind of tickles my fancy. I don't want to laugh, yet it's funny. Lord, please help me to resist temptation today.

"Lord, you know when Satan presents some sex temptation, how weak I am. Please help me, Lord. Give me strength, Lord. Give me wisdom. Give me purity of mind." We moan on and on.

Then, "Lord, today if I have an opportunity for witness, you know how I get nervous and sweaty and I forget all the memory verses. Lord, please help me to witness today. Remind me of the verses."

We begin the morning wailing, groaning, and begging—pleading the Lord to help us. We head out the door wondering whether He heard or didn't hear, or whether or not we did enough begging. We wonder if we're going to "make it" that day.

Sometimes we're more defeated than when we started the prayer. Actually, the way we ought to start each day, since Jesus Christ indwells us, is by praising Him for what He's going to do. We can be realistic in presenting our problems and temptations, but that's not news to the Lord. He's not surprised that temptation comes to us or that we get nervous when we try to witness.

Meet the sun with praise some morning and see if that doesn't start you humming the victor's song as you open the curtains. "Thank You, Lord Jesus, that here's a new day" (even if it is Monday morning). "I thank You, Lord, that even though today will bring temptations, You indwell me and Your power *is* bigger than my temptation. Your strength *is* sufficient to overcome that temptation. Thank you, Lord, that today when the opportunity comes for witnessing, You *will* give me the strength, the words, and the wisdom that I need for that oppor-

46

tunity. Thank You, Lord.

"Thank You that when a sex temptation comes along, *You will* give me the victory, not only in my thought life, but in my will. So that even though I see the temptation and it's very real, in Your power I can simply walk right by and overcome that temptation.

"Thank You, Lord Jesus, that this is going to be a great day because I know that You live in me and Your power, Your wisdom, and Your resources are more than enough for all my needs today."

That's the way to start the day! This isn't just positive thinking, which could be psychological. It is simply acting on the truth of Scripture. Christ does live in me. Because of that, "I can do all things in him who strengthens me" (Philippians 4:13).

This knowledge gives a freedom and spontaneity to the Christian life. It is the wide open gate to the Christian's "promised land." Can you imagine being able to face temptations, not in a nervous, jittery way, but being able to say, "Certainly I've got temptations. I'm human. The Lord knows I'm tempted.

"But I also have Jesus Christ at the core of my inner self, radiating His power and purity. When temptations come, I possess everything that He is and it's enough to overcome anything that may come against me."

This realization makes the Christian life a free life —an exciting life. We can walk out and face the world, not in our own strength, but in His almighty power; not with imagined resources that aren't really there, but in the fulness of everything that

Jesus Christ is.

> *See to it that no one makes a prey of you by philosophy and empty deceit, according to human tradition, according to the elemental spirits of the universe, and not according to Christ. For in him the whole fulness of deity dwells bodily, and you have come to fulness of life in him, who is the head of all rule and authority (Colossians 2:8-10).*

Jesus Christ is God. Everything that God is, Jesus Christ is. Everything that God has, Jesus Christ has. Where is Jesus Christ? In me. In you. All the resources of God are available to me as a Christian, right now and every moment of the day. In Christ is all the fulness of God and Christ dwells in me. Therefore, I have come to *fulness of life* in Jesus Christ.

The thing that makes the Christian life thrilling, powerful, clean, and fully satisfying is not our dedication, but His presence in us.

When we understand this, that He really indwells us in all His fulness, and all we need do is allow Him to take the steering wheel in our lives, then we begin to move into the promised land—the spiritual promised land with all its blessings. We can enjoy the milk and honey and victory in the midst of the battle.

STOP STRUGGLING

It takes many of us so long to learn this basic fact. And for some reason, the more educated we are, the longer it takes us to learn it. An educated person many times finds it hard to admit that there is anything he cannot do if he just puts his mind to it.

We like to believe that if we put our minds to it and apply ourselves, we'll make it, and that we don't need Christ in the day's affairs. So we go on year after year, imagining that someday we'll assemble the puzzle pieces of life on our own. All the while Christ is patiently saying, "Let Me do it for you. Stop struggling. Stop killing yourself. I will make you the kind of man or woman that you ought to be and that you really long to be, but that you'll never be, until you let Me do it for you."

We must allow Him to work in us. The first step is to truly believe that the Son of God in all His fulness dwells within us. Unfortunately, this may take a long time.

I used to think, when the Bible speaks of Christ "coming into" a life, that it was a figure of speech, explained so children would understand. The phrase has become such a cliché in Christian circles that the awesome impact of its implications hardly moves us anymore.

What a terrible mistake. It isn't a figurative thing. It's real. It isn't just a way of speaking. It is the very heartbeat of truth. This is one of the deepest mysteries of the universe that the living God could inhabit a human spirit—my spirit, your spirit.

If you've not asked the Lord Christ to be your own Savior, if he does not fill your spirit—someone else does. And I hate to tell you who that is. No matter who you are, if you have not invited Christ in, you are a child of the devil. And so you will remain—eternally—until Jesus Christ comes in.

Have you unbolted your heart and thrown open the door to Him? Are you sure? Who is the indweller of your life—right now?

Now is the moment to face the walls that have kept you from the land of promise—now is the moment to surge forward in His Name and lay claim to the golden promises engraved with your name. Life is too short to waste precious years in the desert.

3

"I Didn't Come to Take Sides . . ."

Some of the very first enemies the children of Israel had to face in the Promised Land were very personal enemies and it wasn't the "giants" of the land they were confronting. It was themselves. It's always this way, for often we feel our problems are caused by our neighbors, our friends, or members of our family.

Someone may ask us, "How come you're such a defeated Christian?"

"Well, if my wife were more spiritual, I'd be all right," we reply. We blame "that woman (or that man) I married." Or perhaps it's our mother-in-law or our boss. We're ready to blame anyone except ourselves.

Unless we begin where the children of Israel had to begin, we'll never overcome the troubles and problems in our personal lives.

A SURRENDERED HEART

Before the Israelites were ready to confront the "out there" enemies, they had to face some personal, inward matters much nearer home. One of the first commands the Lord gave them after they had entered the land was that all men had to be circumcised (Joshua 5:2-9). Just what does this act of circumcision signify? We've read that word in the Bible so many times.

We know what it is physically, literally, but what is the spiritual meaning of this strange rite? God seems to have chosen this ceremony to bring out an important lesson. I don't fully understand why the Lord would use circumcision to teach one of the most profound spiritual lessons, but there it is.

Actually, circumcision speaks to us about dealing with the self-life, the flesh, the ego. It speaks of a *surrendered heart*.

These people had been wandering in the desert for forty years and had never obeyed God's command to be circumcised. Can you imagine? Forty years of stubborn insubordination. That was one of the strong, visible reasons why they were forced into four decades of desert vagrancy.

> *"Though all the people who came out had been circumcised, yet all the people that were born on the way in the wilderness after they had come out of Egypt had not been circumcised. For the people of Israel walked forty years in the wilderness, till all the nation, the men of war that came forth out of Egypt, perished, because they did not hearken to the voice of the LORD"* (Joshua 5:5-6).

All of the men in the Israelite camp were supposed to undergo this operation. To the Israelites, this was the sign of their surrender and of their covenant with God. It is also a picture of a Christian's finally coming to grips with his own innate selfishness, his self-glory, and his self-effort in attempting to follow God's will. One has to come to the end of himself. (Study Romans 2:25-29).

Few things are more humiliating to an adult man than to be circumcised. In the Middle-East, even more so. Therefore we understand this rite to demonstrate self-humbling, self-surrender, and brokenness before God. Most of the Arabs do not practice circumcision while Israeli men still do. The Arabs think that being circumcised is a hilarious joke —that there is no reason for such a thing. As a matter of fact, on a world-wide basis, the Jews and the Americans are basically the only ones who do follow this custom.

Coming back to the spiritual implications of this unusual object lesson—if you say that the ego must be crucified with Christ, most people laugh and ask, "Who can live that way?"

If you say, "I am crucified with Christ," people say, "You're out of your mind. Don't be so literal — you can't be crucified. You have to *live*. You have to assert yourself. Don't let people push you around. Don't let them step all over you. If you're going to be a strong Christian, you'd better get down to sweating and really working at it or you'll be defeated. God helps those who help themselves." Right?

Looking further in Joshua Chapter 5, we note a second vital, inward matter that the Israelites had to settle.

While the people of Israel were encamped in Gil-

*gal they kept the passover on the fourteenth day
of the month at evening in the plains of Jericho
(Joshua 5:10).*

After a lapse of many years, the Israelites cele-
brated the Passover of the Lord. The Passover
speaks to us of a *thankful heart.*

"Lord, thank You. We're finally across Jordan
into this great good land which You have given to
us. Now we enter the promised life of victory,
abundance, and joy. Lord God, thank You."

NEW FOOD IN A NEW LAND

There was to be a third new experience in that
first eventful week west of the Jordan:

*"And on the morrow after the passover, on that
very day, they ate of the produce of the land, un-
leavened cakes and parched grain. And the
manna ceased on the morrow" (Joshua 5:11-
12).*

You remember that for forty years as they wandered in the desert, every day—for breakfast,
lunch, and dinner they had only one kind of food—
manna (Exodus 16:1-36). Many of them complained
for years and years. But it was necessary that they
eat such a skimpy meal three times a day, because
of their own rebellion.

I remember the time when I didn't know and
hadn't experienced for myself what it means to
have Christ controlling my life. Even though I
wanted to serve God, I was walking in the flesh —

54

"wandering in the wilderness." Sometimes when a preacher would read a passage from the Bible, Ephesians 6, for instance, I'd say, "Oh, no. Not that 'whole armor' thing again. I've heard that stuff since I was in diapers."

Or they'd read about the prodigal son and I'd say, "Oh, spare me, not the prodigal and the pig pen again. I've heard a million and seven sermons on that one." (Yawn.)

As a matter of fact, there was very little that sounded new or fresh or alive to me. It all seemed like the same old thing—manna, manna, manna. Every preacher sounded just like the last dull bore to step behind the pulpit. When you are wandering in the desert of self-effort and trying to please God in your own strength, you're just feeding on the basics, on the bare minimum. It can get pretty boring. God intended it to be pretty boring because He never intended that we stay in the wilderness.

If he fed us steak in the desert, we'd never develop a hunger for the Promised Land. Being satisfied with less, we'd never move into His best. Hebrews 5 says we ought to move on from the basic things of Christianity—the manna and the milk. It's all right for babies, it's fine for spiritual ulcers, but God wants us to move on to solid food! Have some meat for a change! Get your teeth into a spiritual T-bone!

While the children of Israel tented in the barren wastes, God provided them with a steady diet of manna—forty years of it! However, the day after they crossed the Jordan, they were to begin drawing their provision from the land itself. Cut off from

55

stubborn self-effort, surrendered in heart, worshiping God, and celebrating their redemption, they began to eat the good things of the Promised Land. They began to enjoy the fruits of victorious living.

A Christian doesn't begin to enjoy the things of Scripture until he finally understands that Christ lives in him; that God isn't expecting him to be a spiritual giant, out of sheer self-effort, dedication, long hours of prayer, and lots of Bible study; that all God expects of him is to allow the indwelling Christ to control and fill and direct him.

Until we come to that place, we may know the Bible backwards and forwards and yet be a spiritual bore. We may know all the dispensations and be able to debate with anyone, yet feel empty and dry and basically (if one were honest) sick of the whole thing. That's the way I used to feel.

The Scripture tells me that I deserve that. If you're in that position, you deserve it too. However, you don't have to stay there, *not one more day*. You can get out of the spiritual desert and cross the spiritual Jordan and begin to enjoy the new spiritual life.

What a change it makes. Everything becomes new. The old Biblical passages come alive. Of course, you're a child of God before you make that move, but now you're not munching manna.

JOSHUA FACES HIMSELF

Israel's preparation for battle was still not complete. Before they could face the enemies in the land, there was a fourth preliminary inward step with which Joshua, as their leader, had to contend. This final issue was the question of supremacy. It is always the final question and must be settled before there can be any progress at all. Who was Master in Israel? Who was Lord? Who was in charge of the host? Who was to command? Visualize this unusual scene:

> When Joshua was by Jericho, he lifted up his eyes and looked, and behold, a man stood before him with his drawn sword in his hand; and Joshua went to him and said to him, "Are you for us, or for our adversaries?"
>
> And he said, "No; but as commander of the army of the LORD I have now come."
>
> And Joshua fell on his face to the earth, and worshiped, and said to him, "What does my lord bid his servant?"
>
> And the commander of the LORD's army said to Joshua, "Put off your shoes from your feet; for the place where you stand is holy." And Joshua did so (Joshua 5:13-15).

I CAME TO TAKE OVER

Just before they go to face Jericho and all the other outward enemies that they will have to fight in order to take over the Promised Land, suddenly Joshua comes face to face with the Lord Himself.

Joshua, as many of us would do in facing the Lord (for this "man" of verse 13 is obviously the Lord), asks, "All right, whose side are you on, my side or the other?"

The Lord replies, "Joshua, I didn't come to take sides. *I came to take over.*" Did you notice verse 14? "As commander of the army of the Lord I have now come." Then Joshua gets it. Falling at the feet of the Lord, he says, "What does my lord bid his servant?"

Now Joshua is ready to take on Satan, Jericho, Ai —any and all the enemies. Finally he catches on. Ray Stedman says, "We cannot have God's power for our program or for our plans, but He must have us for His plans."

Joshua was before the Lord. "Lord, are You on my side or the other? I have a plan, Lord. I'm going to take over this land. I have my sketches ready."

He's been standing there studying the situation, planning this crusade against Jericho, never bothering to talk to the Lord. He's not on his knees, but on his feet. The Lord wants him on his face.

In the land of Egypt, Joshua may have been a military man. He was probably well acquainted with battle strategy, attack plans, and modern equipment. He was Moses' number one assistant. Now, here he was before the Lord. What a stroke of good luck, he thinks. Here's the perfect opportunity to impress Him with my battle plan.

"Lord, listen to this. Take a look at these sketches —they're really good. See, we can send two divisions over the wall with ladders; two divisions are going to tunnel under; then one platoon is going to be catapulted right over the top!

"Clever, right? All the latest techniques known to modern warfare. By the way, whose side did You say You were on? You *are* on our side, aren't You?"

There he is, with all his charts and graphs spread out in the sand, all his textbooks on Egyptian warfare that he'd checked out from Pharaoh's library and forgotten to return.

"Now all you have to do, Lord, is read over these —just skim them—and sign at the bottom. . . ."

But the Lord had come to take over! What a shock for Joshua. Yet it was the healthiest thing that could have happened to him, of course, because he then fell flat on his face and said, "What does my Lord command of His servant?"

It wasn't really Joshua who won the victories in Canaan, was it? It was the Lord who took over, and it was the Lord working *in* Joshua and *through* him. It's the same with us in our spiritual battles, once we understand the principle that "Christ lives in us."

Yet, for some reason, we would rather spend hours and hours at breakfast meetings, at planning tables, and in business sessions than flat on our face before the Lord. It's so undignified to be in that position, isn't it? Such a waste of valuable time. Oh, how foolish I still am, even after all these lessons and all these years.

But Joshua would have remained camped at Gilgal and would never have progressed another step toward victory, if he had not spent time on his face, acknowledging the sovereignty of his Commander in chief.

When we're first converted, we boastingly say, "Man, I'm going to convert my mother-in-law if it kills me. I'm going to convert all my neighbors, my boss, and that old drinking partner that I used to have. I'm going to quit my job and go to seminary. I'm going to become a minister. Look out, world. Look out, sinners. Here I come!"

We're so full of excitement, we see all the glorious possibilities, and we think that we can do it on our own. Sooner or later we must come to the experience that Joshua had right there—in the dust before Jericho. We must come face to face with our Lord Jesus Christ and say, "Lord, not my plans, but *Yours*. I'm not going to borrow Your indwelling power to do what I want to do. I thank You for Your indwelling power. Now, Lord, what are You going to do through me?"

This makes all the difference. I know of many people who have become missionaries. I happen to be a missionary evangelist myself. I am certain that the Lord wants me where He's got me right now; however, I've met many missionaries who have left the field defeated.

One couple I know went to Haiti and it didn't work out. They came back home. They went to Colombia and it didn't work out. They came back. When I went to their home some months ago, the husband said to me, "I wish that Christian colleges wouldn't emphasize missions so much. They give you the impression that if you're a missionary you're spiritual and that if you're not a missionary you're carnal. I went out thinking that I was going to be God's champion in Haiti and the Lord just dragged me back home.

"Then my family and I went to Colombia and we almost died there. We went through language school and couldn't grasp the language. We were sick, we had many troubles. The Lord had to drag us back home.

"After wasting eight years we were so defeated that my wife and I asked the Lord, 'Lord, what's going on? We're trying to serve You. We're so desperate to be Your servants. We went out and You just sent us home defeated, broken, sick. We lost a child, and it was hell.'

"You know what the Lord told us?" he continued. "He said, 'I never asked you to be a missionary. You took off on your own. You never bothered to spend time with Me. You took off and came back, then took off and came back. Now, after eight years, when you're really broken and flat on your face, now you ask, "Lord, what's happened?"

" 'What's happened is that you never bothered to spend time with Me asking Me what I wanted you to do.' "

Today my friend is teaching school. Every time I see him he tells me, "Luis, I am so happy here. I *know* that God wants me teaching in this Christian school. I've won kids to the Lord. I've had camps. I take guys out on fishing trips and have won many of them to Christ. God wanted me here all the time while I was killing myself trying to do what I thought I should do for God."

We've all made that mistake, although this example is a little more dramatic than most. And this is what the Lord is teaching Joshua here. "I didn't come to take sides with you, Joshua. I came to take over! If you let Me take command, you'll conquer Jericho, Ai, and Gilgal, and take over the whole land. But if you refuse to put Me in command, you

61

are going to lose it all."

Fortunately, Joshua said, "Lord, tell me what to do! Your servant is right here." That's the way we should respond, too.

If you find yourself in serious trouble, the kind of trouble that reveals that you're not allowing Christ to control your life, come to Him and say, "Lord, am I having these troubles because I haven't spent time asking for your direction? Just running off on my own, doing what I think that I should do?"

How long since you have come face to face with the lordship of Jesus Christ in your life? How long have you waged your own campaigns, mapped your own strategy, waged your own battles? Consider these things if you find the Enemy has backed you against the wall. Paul said,

> *For though we walk in the flesh, we do not war after the flesh: (for the weapons of our warfare are not carnal, but mighty through God to the pulling down of strong holds) (2 Corinthians 10:3-4 KJV).*

Jesus Christ is more than a Savior; He is Supreme Commander. And He is holy.

> *And the commander of the LORD's army said to Joshua, "Put off your shoes from your feet; for the place where you stand is holy." And Joshua did so (Joshua 5:15).*

"You shall be holy, for I am holy," says the Lord. What a sight to have observed! God is there! The great General Joshua on his face before his Almighty Commander in chief: God Himself. Off go

Joshua's shoes—this is holy ground. This matter of lordship is no laughing matter. It is solemn stuff, Joshua. None of this playing rebellious games before the Lord God. Take those shoes off.

This is a holy affair!

First, the Lord establishes Himself as Commander. Second, He says, "I have *now* come." Now, now, now! Not tomorrow, not sometime. Now! This is the moment.

Does this awesome scene remind you of Saul of Tarsus falling off his mule on the Damascus road in Acts 9? Does it remind you of Peter on his knees exclaiming, "Depart from me, for I am a sinful man, O Lord" (Luke 5:8)?

Better still, does this remind you of a very personal encounter at some point in your own life? Have you ever, with a sense of finality, fallen on your face and asked—no conditions attached— "What does my Lord bid His servant?"

This scene should run a sharp hook right into your heart. Have you ever been gripped by the awesome holiness of your God? Has it ever drawn you irresistibly to your knees? Have you, then, fallen to the dust—to the floor—on your face—in personal humiliation and brokenness before God? Joshua did and Joshua was never the same. Neither were the walls of Jericho.

Why not bow before your almighty Commander in chief right now. Wherever you are. Whoever you are. The Lord says to you, "I haven't come to join your side. I have come to be your King. I have come to take over, *now*."

This is the moment. Let Him do it.

On your face!
Now!

4

The Outworking
of the Indwelling

Lying on his face in the dirt before the Lord, Joshua found himself asking an appropriate question. It was, in fact, the only question he could have asked in that situation.

"What does my lord bid his servant?"

Joshua realized it was the Lord Himself who confronted him, sword drawn, before the city of Jericho. If it had been an angel, he would have no authority to ask anyone to take his shoes off, because an angel is another created being. But recognizing the Commander of the Lord's Army for who He really was, Joshua kicked off his sandals and fell to the turf in worship.

"Oh God, what do You want me to do?"

Blinded by a great, burning light that paled the noonday sun, Saul of Tarsus would ask the same question centuries later.

And it is the question we must ask as well. Once we've taken the first step and found that "Christ lives in me," the proper question is, "Now, Lord, what would you have me to do?"

How do I begin to navigate? How do I actually allow the indwelling Jesus Christ to make His promises practical in my day-to-day living? How does it work?

Everywhere I go, in Latin America and even in the United States, people will ask, "How does Christ help in the daily life? How does He actually do it?" And what we must realize is this: it isn't just a nice doctrine, a very attractive truth, an interesting, lovely thought that Christ lives within us. It works. *He works.*

I believe that each person has to begin to discover for himself, in personal intimacy with His Lord, how Jesus Christ can take over in his life. The Bible lays down some principles on how He wants to do it.

We must learn to walk with Him, and we must allow Him to deal with us on a deep, personal level in order to grow into a functioning faith. We don't want just a good theoretical faith, though that is good, or even a good, clear understanding of these things. We want our faith to function, don't we? We want it to work, pragmatically. We want it to work because we need it and because we want others to see it, to understand it, and desire it for themselves.

Our question is: what *is* God trying to do with me? What *did* Jesus Christ come to live in me? What is He trying to do with my life? Why didn't He simply turn me loose, saying, "Look, friend, I'm going to save you; I'm going to take you to heaven a little later. Meanwhile, just do the best you can. Here are the Ten Commandments. Try hard. Do your best. Do quite a bit of praying. Find your own way; and when you die you'll come to heaven, and it'll all be settled." What was the real reason that He came to indwell us?

I believe the most important reason, apart from the fact that it's for God's glory, is found in Romans 8:28 and 29:

> *We know that in everything God works for good with those who love him, who are called according to his purpose. For those whom he foreknew he also predestined to be conformed to the image of his Son, in order that he might be the firstborn among many brethren.*

That's God's purpose for your life and for mine. What is God trying to do with your life? He seeks to conform you to the image of His Son. In other words, He wants to build in us *His* character. As we mature and as He controls us day after day, week after week, our mate, our children, our neighbors, and our friends will be able to see that year after year there's a little bit more of Jesus Christ evident in our life. That's the purpose for which He saved us.

He'll never be finished with us on this earth. He's going to perfect us when He comes at the Day of Jesus Christ (Philippians 1:6) when finally, we'll all be completely adapted to His character. But, meanwhile, He is developing us in this direction. Have you seen any growth in the past year along these lines in your personal character? Has there been *something* of the image of Christ formed in you, so that your wife or husband can actually see His reflection in your actions and attitudes? It is good when someone can say to you, "You know, since I saw you last, you've really grown." That's great! It ought to be evident. It ought to be visible, eventually, that the image of Christ is focusing daily in greater definition and clarity within your personality.

Though we may not be able to take someone to the blackboard and diagram Christ's growing impact within us, we may nevertheless go right on enjoying the triumph and the sweet fruit of that relationship as we learn. This is part of God's faultless, compassionate plan.

Victory is immediately available to all of us. That does not imply, however, that we are mature Christians. It simply means that we are under the lordship of Christ, and that we are available to Him to bring us through the maturing process. There's a difference between living under His control, therefore being victorious Christians, and understanding the mysteries of Christ.

Very few of us are poets. I couldn't even write love poetry when I was dating my wife. I tried. The heart was there but the pen wouldn't cooperate.

"Face it," I told myself, "You'll never be Luis Longfellow." I wanted to think that there was a poet inside me just waiting to peck through his shell and woo the world. But it wouldn't happen! The shell was too tough.

So I didn't write much about love, but I experience love. I can't explain it, but I enjoy it. I really love my wife and I know she loves me. We can't write about it, we can't explain it, but we certainly experience it.

In Latin America, I know of many, many Christians who are poorly educated—barely literate — but they know the Lord Jesus. They love Him, they enjoy Him, and their lives sing with His victory. It is no great task to see flashes of His character —His tenderness and His love—in their lives. The mark of the Savior is there! Yet, for all of this, they are not very mature. They couldn't begin to explain to you what they're experiencing in Jesus Christ or why.

How long is the list? There are many, many things that we cannot explain about this mystery of the indwelling Christ. We are so eager (I read every book I can get on the subject), trying to understand more and more and more. What about the "old man" and the "new man" and the Holy Spirit and Jesus Christ? Who is it that actually indwells me, the Spirit or Christ or both? When is it Christ and when is it the Spirit?

There are a million questions. We feel like children splashing ever so gingerly on the edge of the gentle surf. We pick up a shell, trace in the wet sand, or squint our eyes at the blue horizon; but there is a whole ocean before us. Can we fill our plastic buckets with a little sand and water and say we know the sea?

All of our questions are not resolved and will not be resolved! 1 Corinthians 13 says, "Now we know in part . . ." and "now we see through a glass, darkly. . . ." And we shall know in part until that day when we see Him, *but we can grow*. There's a big difference between knowing and experiencing. We can experience the fulness of Jesus Christ without being able to explain it, theoretically and theologically.

Doesn't that encourage you? It ought to. All Christ asks from us is that we put our faith to work.

As someone has accurately put it, "Obedience is faith in action." After I recognize that the Son of God is the center of my life, I may say, "Yes, I believe it," but I truly believe it when there is evidence of obedience in my life. When I begin to operate on a basis of what He tells me in His Word by the power of the Holy Spirit, then I am truly trusting Him. Until then, even though it may be good, solid doctrine, it's just theory, it's just head knowledge. It isn't real for me.

Normal Relationship

The relationship we have with the indwelling Jesus Christ is a normal relationship. It's as normal as my relationship with my wife, only on another level—a spiritual, supernatural level. But I know it's a normal relationship to the Lord, because there He is, day after day, when I'm asleep and when I'm awake. Jesus Christ is right there.

When I'm gone from my wife, as I am so much, my relationship to her is perfect. I don't yell or bang the door when I leave. Usually I leave in good spirits with no quarrels between us. Once in awhile I've left with something between us, and I've had to write a letter quickly and ask her to forgive me for being so silly or mean to her before we parted.

But I'm not thinking about my wife ceaselessly throughout the day. I'm not thinking, "Pat, Pat, Pat," all the time. No, because I can't do that. Yet, I'm still married to her, we're still one, we love each other, and we're in perfect harmony. Even when we're 3,000 miles away from each other, the relationship continues. When we see each other again, it goes on, just as if no physical, geographical interruption had occurred. But I don't have to be thinking about her every minute. I don't have to be talking to her or holding hands with her all the time to be able to say that she and I are in perfect harmony and that we understand each other.

It's the same with the indwelling Jesus Christ. I'm not concentrating on the reality of His presence every moment of the day, but deep down I'm depending on it. I don't have to be constantly thinking "Oh, Lord, Lord, Lord." He's there, and I know He's there, and there's nothing between us. If I'm doing what He's led me to do and what I know I should be doing, well, He's doing it and I'm doing it. We're doing it together. There's no sense of separation; and yet at times, there's no conscious sense of His presence.

Now, if at some given moment I have a little time or there's a problem, I turn to Him and there He is. I can say, "Lord, thank you for this; that was great," or "Lord, I'm going to need wisdom." I talk to Him, and then it becomes conscious. But He and I are in a perfect, harmonious relationship which is never broken unless I consciously disobey Him.

If that happens, then I lose my peace and something inside tells me, "Luis, it isn't right." I get that uneasy feeling. It's exactly the same for all of us who are married when something's wrong. Maybe we don't say anything, but the air is a little tight. We're in the same house and we meet in the hallway or she comes up the stairs and I come down, but there's a little "electricity" there. Maybe we speak, but there's an "ummmm" sort of vibration that you can't quite explain. Either in one or both of our hearts, the love song is off key. The harmony isn't quite there. So what do we have to do? We settle it before the static leaves the house, and then the harmony is achieved.

The moment you clear it up, everything's fine again. There is forgiveness, even if you don't go around kissing each other and saying, "Oh, oh, forgive me." We see this in our walk with Christ. His attitude toward us never changes. He's always loving, always self-giving, always most eager to have a perfect relationship with us. It's always we who cause the problems. Therefore, the moment the Holy Spirit points out a weakness and we ask for forgiveness, we are forgiven and the fellowship begins all over again.

No one else really knows the condition of my relationship to the Lord Jesus. Sometimes my associates or my family can sense if it has deteriorated to a great extent, but most of the time people can't actually tell.

This brings us back to our husband and wife illustration. You can put on a front, sit together and act as if you're getting along; but, when you get back home—"Grrrr"—you begin to snap at one another again. You can impress others outside; but inwardly you're thinking, "Yeah, we're holding hands for the benefit of all the onlookers, but I'm going to deal with you when we get alone."

When we are in a perfect relationship with the indwelling Jesus Christ, several things begin to happen normally and naturally. Sometimes on a conscious level and sometimes on an unconscious level, the Spirit of God and Jesus Christ begin to work through us.

"You Shall Be As My Mouth"

One of the first things is that we become, to use a phrase in Jeremiah 15:19, as the mouth of God.

> *Therefore thus says the LORD: "If you return, I will restore you, and you shall stand before me. If you utter what is precious, and not what is worthless, you shall be as my mouth. They shall turn to you, but you shall not turn to them. And I will make you to this people a fortified wall of bronze; they will fight against you, but they shall not prevail over you . . . says the LORD" (Jeremiah 15:19-20).*

Did you catch the implications of that statement? "If you separate what is precious from what is vile, you shall be as my mouth." Living in this perfect relationship with the indwelling Christ, whenever I speak, when I counsel with someone, or just in everyday conversation, what I say is as the Word of God to that person I'm talking to. There's a power —a purity—an impact in what we say. The other person may not be quite sure what's going on, but he senses something. He's not sure what it is, but something is speaking to him on a deeper level. It's the indwelling Christ, using our personality to reveal Himself and to speak to people.

This may sound mysterious to you. It is mysterious. Life isn't always scientifically explainable.

But, if we are in submission and obedience to our Lord, it pleases Him to use us as His vessels—His ambassadors—in all of our interpersonal conversations and encounters. Jesus Christ lives in me; and, when I speak, although I may not realize it, God is using my words either to touch the other person or to do something for him. It may not be specifically giving him the gospel. It may be just normal conversation in the office or the kitchen or wherever we are. There is a clean, fresh openness in the way we use our words. Something in our expression and our words is different and God uses it to reveal Himself and speak to the needs of those people.

Other scriptures, such as 1 Peter 4:11, emphasize that he who speaks should speak "as the oracles of God." In other words, when we are consciously controlled by Jesus Christ, we speak with an authority that is beyond human authority. You cannot acquire this quality in a Dale Carnegie course. It's supernatural. It is not *you* at all. It comes from another source—the life of the Son of God within you. When an opportunity comes for witness, we don't have to panic and feel our palms begin to sweat because we've got the "Four Spiritual Laws" booklet and we don't know how we're going to use it.

"Uh . . . have . . . uh, you, uh, ever heard of the Four Spiritual Laws, uhh. . . ."

No! You don't have to panic. You may feel the tendency to panic; but you must say, "Wait a minute, little fellow. Now just hold it here. It's not you. Look, if it is you who's going to witness, why not just close the booklet and go for a walk? It's not going to have that much impact."

But if you are trusting the indwelling Jesus Christ, He will use you and the booklet. He will use the Four Laws or He could use the Fifty Laws! Who cares? He's going to speak. He's going to use me. Sensing the presence of God, the person you talk to will be aware that the Spirit of God has a message for him.

Oh, what a relief. You're not leaning your full weight on a snappy outline, saying, "Oh, dear, I don't have a good illustration for that point. Let's see, where's that book of illustrations. Ah . . . oh here . . . let's see . . . sin, sin, sin—oh, here's a good story."

No wonder preachers get bored and leave the ministry. Who wants to go on playing that kind of game? That's not what He has called us to do. When we are moving in His control, living in Him and meditating on the scriptures, there is so much to say that we wonder how to *limit* our remarks to forty minutes. That's the real problem. But not, what shall I say or how shall I work it up?

When God speaks, you can relax. This is what I do. I say, "Well, Lord, I want You to speak tonight, to me as well as to the others. I want You to be in the spotlight, Lord." Sometimes I do find myself struggling through a message and I feel it. I'm sure the audience feels it too, though perhaps they couldn't put their finger on it. They might say, "He didn't sleep well last night," when the real problem is that I'm striving to say something in my own strength from my own resources rather than the Lord's.

A second realization that brings real peace is that God, the Lord Jesus Christ, is also working in all other children of God as He is working in me. He is accomplishing His purpose in His church—the whole Body of Christ. I must learn to trust Jesus Christ to do in my wife what He is doing in me. I need to trust Him to work in that elder of my church as He is working in me. He will do for His Body collectively what He is doing in my personal life individually.

So many times, when we see someone who has a weakness or several weaknesses, our tendency is either to discard that person, to despise him somewhat, or even to mentally criticize him. We find a way to quietly, coolly disregard him. If he leaves the church, we say, "Good riddance. He was no good anyway."

We do this instead of coming to grips with the fact that we are one body in Christ and that even the very weakest Christian has Jesus Christ dwelling within as much as I do. But perhaps he has never understood that life-changing fact. No one has taken the time to teach him. That's why he's living such a miserable, desert-like life. That's why he's going around in circles. That's why he's always thirsty and hungry and out of sorts—fighting, complaining, and being disciplined by the Lord just like the Israelites.

What should I do then? What is my response? I must learn the truth of the verse we quote so often (but seldom really expect), Philippians 1:6: "He who began a good work in you will bring it to completion at the day of Jesus Christ." So, when we find ourselves in a congregation of "carnal" believers who have little understanding of the internal Christ-life, what are we to do?

Panic, right? Throw up our hands and begin to look for another church! What should we do? (I'm talking about a true body of believers—a body where the truth is preached and where the Lord's presence is evident.)

If I truly care as I pretend to care, I'm going to exercise faith in Jesus Christ on behalf of that weak or carnal believer. And I would pray, "Lord, I used to be just like him a few years ago. I remember it so well. Lord, you brought me out of it; and what a difference there is in my life since I understood that you indwell me. Now I'm going to ask you and trust You, since You indwell Joe (or Jill), to do in him what You've done in me—and even more so."

Philemon 5 speaks of "faith . . . toward the Lord Jesus and all the saints." That is a mysterious phrase. Faith in the Lord Jesus Christ *toward* all the saints. What does it mean?

It means that we trust Jesus Christ to do in the other man what He has done in us. Paul tells the Philippians, "He who began a good work in you will bring it to completion at the day of Jesus Christ." He didn't say it about himself; he said it about them. He was trusting Christ to accomplish in the Philippians what Christ had already accomplished in him.

These are the two ways in which the indwelling Jesus Christ begins to form His image in us and begins to operate in us when our relationship with Him is harmonious. "Well, what if it isn't harmonious?" you might ask. "What if something isn't right between the Lord and me? What do I do then?"

First of all, the Lord is going to do something about it. He will point out what it is that is wrong. The Lord doesn't play games with us. He always points out where we went wrong or that we are operating in a wrong way. Then, when He points out that weakness or sin, what must we do? There is a well-known promise of Scripture, "If we confess our sins, he is faithful and just to forgive us our sins, and to cleanse us from all unrighteousness" (1 John 1:9 KJV).

At that very moment, the fellowship is back to normal. We don't have to wait. The moment the problem has been pinpointed and confessed, we are forgiven and cleansed; and we resume our life-giving relationship with the Lord.

And once again I have the confidence that, when I speak, He is speaking; and I trust Him to do in others what He has done in me. This is the harmony of life as a Body—not thinking of myself as one great and growing saint of God, every year a little taller, with more spiritual muscles, until I just overshadow you all. Not that at all! Each individual *must* grow, but grow in relation to the whole body.

This is what it means to thrive and mature in the Christian life—knowing Christ is at work in me and trusting Him to work in others.

5

Don't Wait
until You Understand

One of the most exciting experiences I ever had, when I first started preaching in Argentina, was in a little resort town outside of the city of Cordoba. It was just a little meeting with only about twenty very nice-looking, relaxed, upperclass members—but to me it seemed like twenty thousand.

When the message was over, a medical doctor came up to me and said, "Young man, I really thank you for that message. You looked so excited. I think this really merits some investigation. So, you know what I'm going to do? I'm going to buy a Bible (he didn't have one), and I'm going to read it and really try to understand it. Then, once I really understand it, if it's like you explained, I am going to put my trust in Jesus Christ because I do have some needs."

I was pretty new at this, but the Lord always gives answers—even to beginners if we are trusting Him.

So, I boldly said, "You know, Doctor, what you're going to have to do is put your faith in the Word of God. Then you'll begin to understand it."

"Oh, no," he said, "that's not the way I operate. I've got a scientific mind. First, I want to look at the evidence and really understand it and put it all together. I'll have to see whether it's a workable hypothesis and then I'm willing to try it."

"You'll have to go around the rest of your life trying then, because you'll never understand the gospel message," I told him. "First, you must come by faith and believe it as the Word of God; and then God will quietly begin to teach you, helping you to understand."

God was at work in his heart and life because right there in church someone supplied him with a Bible. He took it home and read it, and the next evening he came to where I was staying to tell me that he had trusted Jesus Christ as his Savior. That night fifteen years ago his life changed, and he's been growing ever since. He's still down there, preaching on weekends and being active for the Lord.

It's the same story with many of us. Too often we look at the promises of God, saying that He will give us victory, that He will provide what we need; and we say, "Yes, but I don't understand it yet." Instead of believing the promises, we want to wait until we understand them. The Scripture says, "The just shall live by faith."

Remember how the Lord had told his followers very plainly, "On the third day I'm going to rise again." But being typical human beings, they didn't believe it. When the Lord Jesus joined the two men on the way to Emmaus, they were so unbelieving they didn't even recognize Him. Even though the Lord was there with them, they didn't believe that this was actually Jesus—raised from the dead. He chided them in Luke 24, "Oh, foolish men, and slow of heart to believe all that the prophets have spoken."

It isn't necessary that we understand everything. All the Lord asks is that we believe. But we refuse to believe. We want to see evidence. It was only as they were reclining at the table and Jesus broke bread before them that their eyes were opened. Suddenly they realized, "Why, this is Jesus!" And then He was gone.

Right away they ran back, all the way to Jerusalem, to tell the disciples, "We've seen the Lord. We've seen the Lord! Now we believe that He has risen from the dead." They did not believe it on the basis of His Word; they only believed it when they saw the resurrected Christ.

Jesus later said to Thomas, "Blessed are those who believe even if they don't see." It isn't that what God says isn't credible. It is! It's a matter of our starting point, our basic premise.

> *Though the fig tree do not blossom,*
> *nor fruit be on the vines,*
> *the produce of the olive fail*
> *and the fields yield no food,*
> *the flock be cut off from the fold*
> *and there be no herd in the stalls,*
> *yet I will rejoice in the LORD,*
> *I will joy in the God of my salvation.*
> *GOD, the LORD, is my strength;*
> *he makes my feet like hinds' feet,*
> *he makes me tread upon my high places.*
> *(Habakkuk 3:17-19).*

Immediately the father of the child cried out and

said, *"I believe; help my unbelief!" (Mark 9:24).*

Victory *is* possible for you and for me *now*, but maturity is a steady thing. It takes time. We may enjoy a banner day through Christ today and tomorrow, but there's still a lot to learn and a lot to grow into. It takes years to mature. "He who began a good work in you will bring it to completion at the day of Jesus Christ" (Philippians 1:6). It doesn't happen overnight. We learn. We spend a lifetime learning. He gives us insight. We know him a little better, just from living with the Lord; and just from living in Him, we begin to know Him. But we don't have to remain a defeated Christian until we understand it all. We'd never be victorious if we waited for that, because we'll never understand it all on this side of heaven.

What God looks for is forward movement. He expects hesitations; but as a good Father, He knows what to bring into our lives to encourage growth. As a human infant must pass through the normal steps of growth—childhood, adolescence, adulthood, so spiritual infants must grow continually, step-by-step and slowly, but always forward. Retrogression in human development is abnormal, and so it is in the Christian's development as well.

Each one of us is personally taught by God. Each one in his relationship with Jesus Christ, in his walk with Christ, is taught in different ways. Perhaps the Lord would use me to teach you one new thought. But the Lord will deal with you through your reading of Scripture and through a thousand different incidents in your life—perhaps through a period of lingering illness, perhaps through a plunge in the stock market. God uses all these things to teach us. As we listen to Him and talk to Him, He teaches us; and our roots entwine their way deeper and deeper into the soil of this supernatural relationship.

No one on his sanctified soapbox or behind a prestigious pulpit has the authority to say, "Okay, here it is. Here's God's 97-point plan for your life. Just sign on the bottom line and pick up your personalized notebook at the door."

Plans are the prerogative of God; obedience is the privilege of His children. It is His and His alone to map our path to maturity. The path is not a set of pre-printed principles. The path is Christ Himself.

"Jesus said to him 'I am the way, and the truth, and the life' " (John 14:6).

There are basic guideposts, of course; and, as the Word of God is faithfully read and studied and proclaimed, we find incalculable help in walking the Christ-walk. But God puts each one of us through different experiences, because He created us individually and knows what it takes to produce growth in our lives. He has the right to work with each one of us within the Body and as individuals the way He wants to, and to teach us according to His desire. As parents we use creative and individual methods to teach each one of our children. So does God!

WHAT DIFFERENCE DOES IT MAKE?

Remember what we've discovered so far about

some of the practical aspects concerning the life of Christ within us? The first thing we noted was that when we talk, if we are in harmony with Him, He is actually speaking through us. There's an impact to what we say. There's a power in our life and in our speech, whether we're teaching a Bible study or preaching or counseling or just talking in everyday conversation. When Jesus Christ is in control of our lives, there's something there that speaks of God and blesses the person who's listening. Sometimes we're aware of that power and sometimes we're not aware of it; but we're usually surprised when we see results.

In the second place, when Jesus Christ is at the controls, we can begin to trust Him on behalf of others. I can trust "Christ-in-my-wife" to do in her life what I'll never be able to do. She's going to have to trust "Christ-in-her-husband" to effect changes in me that she can never accomplish. So often, young people get married and say, "Well, I can see some traits in my husband (or wife) that are pretty unpleasant; but just wait until I'm through. I'll change him."

And then they find out that one doesn't change another person. Your example may help and some suggestions may help if your mate is receptive, but the only one who can really effect changes in a personality is the indwelling Jesus Christ.

One person cannot mold another. For a time you can press someone and get him to submit, but finally either the person objects strenuously or silently rebels and there's a divorce. You cannot impose your will on another person for long. Some personality types allow it; most do not. But the Master Craftsman can mold and change entire personalities in a marvelous way.

Now, let's move on to a third practical way that Christ helps us in our daily lives. You remember in Matthew 5:13-14, the Lord Jesus says, "You are the salt of the earth . . ." and "You are the light of the world. . . ."

We are the salt of the earth because Jesus Christ indwells us, not because we are nicer or more deserving than our neighbors. Salt stops corruption; the presence of an individual who is controlled by Jesus Christ in a neighborhood, in an office, in a school, in a dorm, or most anywhere has the same effect as salt does in stopping corruption. When a true Christian is around, even though he may not realize it, the way he behaves, the way he talks, and the way he thinks makes it possible for him to be the salt in that community or in that group of people. The presence of a person under the power and influence of Jesus Christ stops corruption in any situation as if Christ were present Himself—and He is!

Jesus says, "You are the light of the world." A man or woman or even a child who is controlled by Jesus Christ sheds light on a conversation when it comes to spiritual and moral matters. It isn't that he knows everything about every subject, of course; but, when it comes to spiritual things, a Christian in a group sheds light on that subject. If a conversation turns toward problems in the house, an individual walking with the Lord Jesus Christ has a contribution to make that no one else can, unless that person also has Christ in his heart. We are the light of the world.

We can take courage in the fact that Christ is using us wherever we go. 2 Corinthians 2:14 says, "But thanks be to God, who in Christ always leads us in triumph, and through us spreads the fragrance of the knowledge of Him everywhere."

Wherever we go, in the office, in the home, in the neighborhood, in athletics, in traffic, He is leading us in triumph. Because Jesus Christ is our very life wherever we go, He spreads through us "the fragrance of the knowledge of Him."

It is Christ in us who makes our life a fragrant life. There will be something about us that will affect those who come in contact with us. And many times it is unconscious on our part, for we are not constantly thinking, "Christ is in me, and I am in Christ. I am going to do something here in this room for Christ." No. I'm just myself. But Jesus Christ is in control. As we talk and share and counsel, the Lord is spreading His fragrance through us, because He's there and He loves us and He wants it this way. He wants us to be normal; but in our normality, He is speaking to other people.

No matter what we are doing, whether it's washing dishes in the home or whether it's working at the office or studying or whatever we're doing, if we are empowered and directed by the living Christ, He is being glorified in our life, although we may not realize the implications of this as it is happening. Sometimes this takes a while to learn. We think that God is only doing something through us when we're engaged in "spiritual activity," such as preaching or teaching or singing or praying. It's true that at that time God is doing something, but it's also as naturally true as breathing at other times. It's not what I DO as much as who I AM.

Is This What I Came to Do?

When my wife and I were first married, we went to Colombia, South America, to work with Overseas Crusades. My wife didn't know Spanish because she is from Oregon, so we went to Costa Rica where there is a language school. Our twin boys were nine months old when we arrived. Friends found a house for us and helped us get settled, but they didn't find a maid to help us. So for about three weeks, my wife went to language school every day and I had to take care of the twins.

Now in order to appreciate this situation, it must be understood that Latin men DO NOT touch babies and do not work in the kitchen. Culturally, it is quite unthinkable and I had never changed a diaper in my life. I was the first-born in my family, followed by five sisters. This was a fortunate state of affairs, because my sisters took care of the little ones. I had never come near a dirty diaper.

But then came the first day of my wife's language school and off she went, leaving me and the two little guys to fend for ourselves. Soon the twins started crying so I stuck bottles in their mouths and that helped for awhile. But then there were obviously other matters to attend to. I changed one of them (probably not too well); then I changed the other one and they went to sleep.

Then they did it again. Together. It was a conspiracy! They'd wake up at the same time, they'd start yelling at the same time, and then they would . . . at the same time.

So we lived through the first day and the second, third, and fourth day. Then, one day I had one of them on the bed changing his diapers and I said, "Lord, is this what I came to do as an evangelist in Latin America? I left my home country and instead of preaching and saving souls, here I am changing dirty diapers."

Quietly, the Lord began to say to me, "Now, Luis, you're always telling the wives and the women how they have to trust the Lord in every circumstance and how wonderful it is to have Christ in you in all circumstances. But actually you were limiting it to some circumstances that were pleasing." It was a great lesson. I still don't like to change diapers; but I began to realize that it's possible, even while you're doing that unpleasant task, to be in the will of God.

It isn't a question of constantly talking about spiritual things or constantly being engrossed in Christian work. It's just living. Christ is pleased to live in me even when I'm changing diapers. Christ is there and He's with me. I can be as filled with Him when I'm doing the routine, taking care of the dirty little things of life, as I am when I'm out preaching.

Changing diapers can be a spiritual experience if we realize that the totality of our life is hidden in Christ Jesus. This makes a big difference in life. The Women's Liberation people would be far different if they understood this. Life is composed of work and sweat and tears and a lot of ugly, unpleasant things. But, when we realize that the living God is with us, even in the dirty little jobs, then life begins to take new meaning. This is one of the vital things that will teach us to live in the land of promise. We must understand, wherever we go, no matter what we're doing—that God is leading us always in triumph and through us is spreading the fragrance of the knowledge of Him everywhere. It's not what I do but who I AM.

Christ in us helps us another way. In every circumstance of life, negative or positive, Christ is bigger than each one of those circumstances. We will never face any problem that is bigger than He is. Sometimes we think that we do. Sometimes we wonder if the Lord is going to come through for us. In our lack of trust and confidence we just get all shaken up. We tremble; we panic, but the Lord is bigger than our circumstances.

Someone has said that "we believe God can do anything, and yet we expect Him to do nothing." We believe God can do anything He desires; but when it comes right down to it, we expect Him to do very little. And instead of expecting God to come through for us (when the problems come), we get desperate. We begin to panic. We begin to act like men of the world, men who don't know Jesus Christ. We begin to blame others. We forget that Jesus Christ is with us and in us in the very circumstance in which we find ourselves. So we lose the joy and victory that we might have found in our Lord. When the pressure is on, instead of looking to the indwelling Christ, we begin to point a critical finger at those around us and even express anger and unbelief toward God Himself.

I like the story of Joseph in this regard. Joseph (though he didn't know Christ as we know Him today) experienced and relied upon the presence of God in his life. You'll remember that after his brothers sold him as a slave, the wife of his Egyptian master tried to seduce him. When he refused, he was sent to jail.

It seemed as though life was nothing but one crisis after another for Joseph, and he could have doubted God. He might have said, "Well, Lord, where are all those promises that you made to me? You said that everybody would bow down to me, like the stars were bowing down in my dream. You said that everybody would come and serve me. Now look at me. I'm in jail. My brothers hate me— they sold me as a slave. I've been accused of immorality which I didn't commit. Lord, where are You now?" But he didn't do that at all. When his life was all over, he had the testimony that he had trusted God through all his problems.

Speaking to his brothers when he was about to die, Joseph said, "As for you (his brothers) you meant evil against me; but God meant it for good, to bring it about that many people should be kept alive, as they are today." He's telling his brothers, "When you sold me to that caravan, you meant it for evil; but God meant it for good." This is what we learn as we take up residence in the Promised Land, as we understand that the Spirit of Christ lives within us.

We may go through trouble or perhaps someone we trust accuses us falsely. People distrust us or they begin to suspect us. Pressures begin to mount against us. We're tempted to say, "Lord, why do You allow all this? Why did my brother do this or why did my relatives do that or why did that church member accuse me this way? Why, Lord?" We need to have the attitude of Joseph here, when he says, "You meant it for evil, but God meant it for good."

When we acknowledge the reality of Christ's controlling presence in our daily lives, we may look at circumstances and problems from His perspective. Then we can say, "All things work together for good to them that love God" (Romans 8:28). Though I can't understand how a particular circumstance could work for the good, I'm going to trust and believe Him. Then when it's all over, I'll be able to look back and say, "Ah, I can see how this trouble and this problem actually worked out for the best— not only for me but for other people."

In the case of Joseph, a horrible set of circumstances worked out in such a way that he became number two man in the whole world at that time. It also turned out for good for his own family, as he says, "to bring it about that many people should be kept alive, as they are today" (Genesis 50:20).

When we're going through problems, trials, pressures, and attacks which we don't understand, we must take our stand—"Christ lives in me!" I don't understand how these troubles could come upon me, but I am trusting Jesus Christ who loves me and indwells me. I'm trusting that out of these troubles, tribulations, and trials He's going to accomplish His gracious plan in my life. I may not understand right now, but it's going to be for my own good, for my family's good, and for the good of many other people too.

When Temptation Comes

Here is another question that I am asked, wherever I go in the world. How does Christ who lives in me help me when I have to face temptation? How does Christ actually deliver me when temptation comes? I have found great comfort in 1 Corinthians 10:13, "No temptation has overtaken you that is not common to man. God is faithful, and he will not let you be tempted beyond your strength, but with the temptation will also provide the way of escape, that you may be able to endure it."

Every temptation that comes to us is common to other people. Sometimes we feel that we are tempted beyond others. Sometimes I wonder if I'm not more corrupt than other men since some temptations seem to recur in my life. I wonder if I was born a little more depraved than others. But when I read this verse, I am encouraged to realize that many believers face those same temptations. Perhaps, when you look at some people you say, "Oh, they're so nice. I'll bet they're never tempted." But they are. Just as much as I am, and as much as you are. Maybe a little differently, but temptation comes to all of us.

Some are especially susceptible to sexual temptations, while others are weak when it comes to getting out of any problem by lying. Different ones of us have problems with other kinds of temptations. The question is: how do we actually find in the indwelling Jesus Christ, power to overcome temptation? We need to know the actual point at which Christ "comes alive" in a person's life to deal with this.

We read it in 1 Corinthians 10:13: "God is faithful, and he will not let you be tempted beyond your strength." Now, let me ask you a question. What is our strength before temptation? Christ in us is our strength. Now look at it again. It says, "God is faithful, and he will not let you be tempted beyond your strength." What strength do we have? His strength. The strength of Jesus Christ.

"All right, that's fine," you say. "That's good to know—great news—but how do I escape the temptation?" The verse goes on to say, "But with the temptation (He) will also provide the way of escape, that you may be able to endure it." How? Here's where we come to the "how."

What is the way of escape? How does this powerful almighty Jesus Christ, who lives in my life, help me when temptation comes? The answer I've found is twofold. First, Jesus Christ helps me to think with God, to face temptation with God's thoughts. There's a verse in 1 Corinthians 2 that says, "We have the mind of Christ." Now, how does that work? For instance, let's say that we have a sexual temptation. All of us have sexual temptations and that is normal. God created us as sexual beings and we have temptations.

You've just finished your morning devotions, reviewing the two verses you've just memorized and thinking some wonderful spiritual thoughts. You get dressed, have breakfast, and get in the car. Then suddenly as you are driving down the street, before you know it, you see someone of the opposite sex that is just fantastically attractive. You look and you say, "My, my. This is really something very interesting." Now I think that happens to most of us.

For the moment that's not a temptation. It's just one of God's better flowers walking by. And you admire it. But, if Satan begins to implant thoughts that are beyond just a mere physical attraction and the heart begins to covet, that becomes a temptation. I've got to face it. I can't pass it off, because the mind has an instant replay switch and it all comes back. You've got to do something with that temptation. Or it could be worse! It could be that same very attractive person of the opposite sex is trying to trip you up, trying to draw your attention to do something that isn't proper. This happens too. Let's face it. And that's why there are many divorces even among Christians. People don't get divorced just to live under another roof. They are tempted.

What do you do when temptation comes? First of all, you must be honest. Before God you must say, "Lord, here's a temptation. You see what I see; You know how I feel, Lord. It's very attractive; it's really drawing my attention. But, Lord, I realize that you have given me one woman to be my wife. I really love my wife, and I don't want to be unfaithful. I am very happy with the wife that You gave me; and even though this is a temptation, a very attractive temptation as a matter of fact, I thank You, Lord, that You give me the power to overcome the desire of the moment."

That's the way I do it. That's the way I have tapped the almighty strength of Jesus Christ to give me constant victory when I am faced with the pull of these recurring temptations.

First, we must realize that this person doesn't belong to me.

You say, "What if I'm single? How do I know if she does or doesn't belong to me?"

To begin with, covetousness is never love; therefore, it isn't love when a person feels attracted to another person for purely physical reasons. This attraction where he'd like to investigate a little bit, maybe lay his hands on—that isn't love. When God gives a person the one woman or the one man that He has in mind, both will know it. You don't love a person you've never met before. This is just passion —covetousness.

So the Lord helps us to think properly, to think His thoughts. Yet, even that isn't enough. It isn't really enough to say, "Well, I've got my wife; I shouldn't be coveting. In fact, I don't want to covet." It isn't enough, because the strength of temptation and the power of the flesh can sometimes overwhelm these arguments.

Therefore, secondly, Jesus Christ gives us power to implement that thinking with effective action. In other words, we not only have His mind, we also have His power. We can say, "Lord Jesus, You see the temptation that I'm facing at this moment. It's very real, very powerful. But I thank You that You live within me, and Your power is greater and more effective than the power of this temptation. I thank

You, Lord Jesus, that I will NOT fall. I will not continue coveting." 1 Corinthians says that it is our way of escape, that you may be able to endure the moment of struggle. "Enduring it" doesn't mean to say, "Oh, well, let's just scuttle through it." It means that we actually COME OUT of the moment of temptation—and come out victorious.

What I've discovered is this: when I face temptation, whether it's a sex temptation, a temptation to say something that isn't true to get out of a moment of trouble or whatever other temptation it may be, I find that Jesus Christ can show himself strong in these two areas. He helps me to think straight, with God, and secondly, He helps me implement right thinking with powerful action. Fleeing isn't cowardly in many cases. It's wise. It's common, God-given wisdom.

> *Flee also youthful lusts: but follow righteousness, faith, charity, peace, with them that call on the Lord out of a pure heart (2 Timothy 2:22 KJV).*

When the Bible says, "I can do all things through Christ who strengthens me," where is Christ? He's right here! At that moment of temptation, I don't have to clamor or make a long-distance phone call, saying, "Lord, can You hear me? Oh, I need Your strength, Lord. I'm going through this temptation. Can You hear me? Do You have time to help me?"

No! Christ is as near as my pulse-beat. I can say, "Lord Jesus, here comes this temptation. Thank You that you are here. Thank You that You are almighty. And thank You that at this very moment, the temptation is over because You live in me." That's it. The power of the temptation is broken right there—right then—when we turn it over to the indwelling Jesus Christ.

Romans 6:14 becomes true in your experience when it says, "Sin shall not have dominion over you: for ye are not under the law, but under grace" (KJV). And grace is really Jesus Christ. "Sin shall not have dominion over you." It'll try. Sin will come at you. Temptation will come at you. Satan will come at you. But, it shall not have dominion over you, because Christ is there within.

I'm not under the law. It's not me TRYING to be pure or TRYING to be faithful to my wife or TRYING to be a straight-and-honest businessman. It's a completely different ball game. I'm not under the law, but under grace. And sin will not have dominion over me, because Christ lives in me. He's in control of my life. Sin cannot have dominion over Him.

FLAMINGO LEGS AND ALL . . .

The impact of having God resident in our personality goes even deeper than helping us to face temptation. As we allow Him to work, Christ helps us to resolve certain complexes that may have plagued us for years. On the surface, these "little personality quirks" and sensitivities may seem very trivial; but to the one plagued by them, they often loom like great walls, blocking social and spiritual progress.

I have a friend who stutters every time he begins to speak about Christian things. When he's with a client doing a sales job, he's got the most fluent tongue you've ever heard; but speaking of spiritual things, he stutters. One day he asked me for counsel and we spent nearly three hours together, chatting back and forth.

As we began to open our hearts, it came out that he felt so inadequate, so incapable. "Especially if I'm around a fellow like Dick Hillis or Ray Stedman or one of these giants who seem to know all the Bible," he said. "I can hardly talk. They ask me to give a testimony or share a thought or even say a prayer and I think 'Who am I to stand up and talk?' " And so he would begin to stutter.

Finally I said, "John, you're too concerned about yourself. Forget about what these men may think of you and start speaking in the name of Jesus Christ, Who lives in you. Allow Him to say through you whatever He wants to say."

Slowly he told me, "You know, from the moment I asked you the question, I knew you'd come around to that finally. It really is self-centeredness that has given me this complex."

Although we don't like to admit it, all the complexes we have really stem from selfishness in action. Self-centeredness is the root cause.

I used to have several complexes that I'll mention to show you how silly these things can really be. Yet it isn't silly to the person who has them. I used to think that I had skinny legs. I've been told they're not so skinny, but from up here they look skinny. Whether they were or not wasn't the problem. I thought they were.

In the school that I attended in Argentina, a British school, all the boys had to wear short pants.

We wore these flannel shorts, and the students could really be nasty. They used to taunt me, "Hi, flamingo legs." I've always had this problem about my legs. It's stupid, isn't it? But it didn't seem stupid then. I felt terrible.

Some people have a complex about their nose. They're always talking about their nose. They worry and they touch it and they really never enjoy life because they feel that somehow something's wrong with their nose.

I also used to have a complex about my white hands. Maybe to you that doesn't sound so bad; but in Argentina, most people have a little darker skin —not too dark, but darker than mine. I always had a feeling that somehow I was a sissy because I had terribly white hands.

I learned to live with them like a person learns to live with anything, but the sensitivity was still there, right under the surface.

Once I went to Mexico, to Baja, California, for some ministry. I walked into a local pharmacy for a prescription, putting my hands on the counter as I waited.

The sales girl asked me, "Are you a doctor?"

I said, "No. Why?"

She said, "You've got such white hands."

Oh, boy. I put my hands behind my back. I told myself, "Now, this is a stupid thing. I've got to resolve this thing. Why do I go around feeling foolish?"

Finally, the Lord helped me come to the place where I could say, "Lord Jesus, you made me just as I am. You chose to come and indwell me just as I am, white hands, flamingo legs and all. And so, Lord, I thank You that You live in me, and that You chose to live in me, skinny and pale as I may be."

Now you may say, "That's an awfully simple thing." Listen, there are people who cannot cope with life because of such complexes. I mean that literally there are those who have to go to a psychiatrist over a silly little thing that has disturbed them all their life. Many Christian people never open their mouth to witness because they have some sort of an inferiority complex, which the Lord Jesus Christ could resolve in one minute if they could just understand that all of our complexes are a reflection of self-centeredness.

MY skinny legs, MY white hands, MY big nose, MY fat belly, MY short figure. It's really an expression of the "I" in action. It's pretty disgusting when you see it this way.

The way that Jesus Christ within you will help you resolve these complexes is by teaching you to look to Him and say, "Lord, this does bother me. I am incapable, Lord; but You dwell within me and You are entirely capable of making me a powerful servant of Yours. Lord, I'm not all that I wish I were. I wish I were tall and imposing so I could really look authoritative, but I'm not. I'm short and nobody pays much attention to me. But because You made me this way, I love You and I thank You and I trust You. I'm going to forget ME and allow You to be all and in all."

But this precious treasure—this light and power that now shine within us—is held in a

perishable container, that is, in our weak bod-
ies. Everyone can see that the glorious power
within must be from God and is not our own
(2 Corinthians 4:7 TLB).

This is a very practical, effective way in which the indwelling Christ becomes real to us, the more we understand His presence and allow Him to take over.

Now, as we move into Jericho with Joshua and the children of Israel, we're going to discover more about the principles of how God leads a person day by day—how we can know we're on the right path, walking in the direction God wants us to go.

6

The Moment to Shout!

At last we've come to Jericho, the first big challenge in the Promised Land. Notice how many times in the following verses the ark of the Lord is mentioned. The ark is the vivid symbol of God's living presence among His people.

> Now Jericho was shut up from within and from without because of the people of Israel; none went out, and none came in. And the LORD said to Joshua, "See, I have given into your hand Jericho, with its king and mighty men of valor. You shall march around the city, all the men of war going around the city once. Thus shall you do for six days. And seven priests shall bear seven trumpets of rams' horns before the ark; and on the seventh day you shall march around the city seven times, the priests blowing the trumpets. And when they make a long blast with the ram's horn, as soon as you hear the sound of the trumpet, then all the people shall shout with a great shout; and the wall of the city will fall down flat, and the people shall go up every man straight before him."

So Joshua the son of Nun called the priests and said to them, "Take up the ark of the covenant, and let seven priests bear seven trumpets of rams' horns before the ark of the LORD." And he said to the people, "Go forward; march around the city, and let the armed men pass on before the ark of the LORD."

And as Joshua had commanded the people, the seven priests bearing the seven trumpets of rams' horns before the LORD went forward, blowing the trumpets, with the ark of the covenant of the LORD following them. And the armed men went before the priests who blew the trumpets, and the rear guard came after the ark, while the trumpets blew continually. But Joshua commanded the people, "You shall not shout or let your voice be heard, neither shall any word go out of your mouth, until the day I bid you shout; then you shall shout." So he caused the ark of the LORD to compass the city, going about it once; and they came into the camp, and spent the night in the camp.

Then Joshua rose early in the morning, and the priests took up the ark of the LORD. And the seven priests bearing the seven trumpets of rams' horns before the ark of the LORD passed on, blowing the trumpets continually; and the armed men went before them, and the rear guard came after the ark of the LORD, while the trumpets blew continually. And the second day they marched around the city once, and re-

turned into the camp. So they did for six days.

On the seventh day they rose early at the dawn of day, and marched around the city in the same manner seven times: it was only on that day that they marched around the city seven times. And at the seventh time, when the priests had blown the trumpets, Joshua said to the people, "Shout; for the LORD has given you the city. And the city and all that is within it shall be devoted to the LORD for destruction; only Rahab the harlot and all who are with her in her house shall live, because she hid the messengers that we sent. But you, keep yourselves from the things devoted to destruction, lest when you have devoted them you take any of the devoted things and make the camp of Israel a thing for destruction, and bring trouble upon it. But all silver and gold, and vessels of bronze and iron, are sacred to the LORD; they shall go into the treasury of the LORD."

So the people shouted, and the trumpets were blown. As soon as the people heard the sound of the trumpet, the people raised a great shout, and the wall fell down flat, so that the people went up into the city, every man straight before him, and they took the city" (Joshua 6:1-20).

Then let's look at the New Testament account of the story.

"By faith the people crossed the Red Sea as if on dry land; but the Egyptians, when they attempted to do the same, were drowned. By faith

*walls of Jericho fell down after they had been en-
circled for seven days. By faith Rahab the harlot
did not perish with those who were disobedient,
because she had given friendly welcome to the
spies" (Hebrews 11:29-31).*

FAITH BROUGHT DOWN THE WALLS

The writer of the book of Hebrews emphasizes
the historical fact of the fall of Jericho and that it
happened, not because of a fantastic, well-executed
attack by the people of Israel, but by faith. The walls
of Jericho fell down after the Israelites had encircled
them for seven days.

The conquest of Jericho is one of the Bible's most
famous stories because it's so dramatic. It has been
so popularized by the spiritual that says, "Joshua fit
the battle of Jericho," that we take it as almost a
joke. But what happened at Jericho really happened, and the story has a pointed application for
Christians as well. From its mention again in Hebrews 11, we know that it's an illustration; it is a
graphic, action-portrait of the principles that we are
to live by, if we're going to walk by faith.

The Bible tells us that not only do we become
Christians by faith and that Christ comes into our
lives by faith, but it teaches that we must live by
faith. "Now the just shall live by faith" (Hebrews
10:38a KJV).

But how do you do it? Faith seems like such a
nebulous concept, doesn't it? To most people, faith
is somewhat like a cloud. "Faith. Great thing to
have . . . but how do you get it? And how is it pos-

sible to operate by faith?" It seems like something up in the air, something hard to analyze. How does one function by faith?

Here in Joshua we have one illustration of how to operate by faith. The children of Israel are facing a formidable barrier to the land of victory. All the land belonged to them, but in order to move in, it was necessary to conquer Jericho. God told them, "All right, you are going to take this city. As a matter of fact, I'm going to take this city and allow you to participate in the conquest. All you have to do is follow My directions, and Jericho is yours."

The first things to notice here are the rules of action necessary to live by faith. We see them in this story very clearly. How did God enable these people to take over this awesome fortified city of Jericho?

Someone has jokingly said that if a tenor hits a certain note, it'll crack a glass of crystal; therefore, they say that the walls of Jericho came down because, after all that plodding around it and the primitive way they built walls in those days, just the shouting—the very vibrations—brought it down. Not a chance. Those walls were probably 30 to 50 feet wide and nearly 100 feet high! No amount of vibration could crumble that wall. God removed the wall.

THE FIRST RULE

The first rule of action the Israelites had to follow to be able to overtake this tremendous city was this —they had to find out the will and the word of God for that situation. This was the first step.

> *And the* LORD *said to Joshua, "See, I have given into your hand Jericho, with its king and mighty men of valor" (Joshua 6:2).*

God had a plan. When Joshua heard what God had to say, he had quite a surprise. Can you imagine what an incredible plan of action this must have seemed to a military man?

Imagine if the modern day Israeli Defense Command would decide to fight its battles in the same way Joshua was required to fight Jericho! We might compare this to using BB guns against jet planes. But God said, "This is the way I want you to take the city. It may sound ridiculous to you, but I want you to walk around the city once a day. Everyone must be very quiet. Let the trumpets blow and send the ark of the Lord and the soldiers in front with the people behind. Walk around the city and go back to the camp for six days straight. Then, on the seventh day, go around the city seven times, doing exactly the same thing. But this time, when you hear the trumpet and when Joshua calls, 'Shout!' all of you will shout as loud as you can. The moment you shout, the city walls will fall flat. Every one of you walk straight ahead. Do what you've got to do and take the city over."

Now, that was God's plan of action.

WHAT DOES GOD HAVE TO SAY ABOUT YOUR JERICHO?

Their responsibility was to find out what God

wanted them to do and how God wanted them to do it. Today, you and I, as a Church and as individuals, face the same situation over and over. There are "Jerichos" in our lives. There are Jerichos for the Church. Yet too many people get desperate and discouraged over the Jerichos that they face; and each man takes off on his own with his own puny little plan, trying to solve his problems or those of the church.

People wring their hands—they're worried and they don't know what's going to happen.

One says, "Why don't we do this?"

Another says, "Let's do that."

Somebody else states, "This is the way to act. Let's evangelize in this manner."

Some people say, "The only way to do it is to become politically active."

Others say, "Forget that. Let's just do it the old way."

Everyone gives an opinion.

But it seems that few people are spending time listening to the Lord, trying to discover what He wants, what He expects of us. How does He expect us to live in this day? How does He want us to solve our problems and overcome the Jerichos that we face?

Within the United States, there seems to be a deep undercurrent of concern among Christians concerning the trend of public school education. Many feel that academic and moral standards in our schools have plunged to a new low and these people feel greatly concerned about their children's education. We ought to be concerned. How do you solve the problem? It is good to organize committees and campaigns. It is good to become involved and to send around petitions. But how many of us are spending time before God, pouring out our heart's concern and perplexity before Him? How many of us are asking Him how He wants to see this situation resolved?

OBSTACLES MEAN OPPORTUNITIES

Whenever the Lord presents an obstacle, it is also an opportunity. Jericho was both. It was an opportunity to prove God—and the walls were very real!

Now, they did not face a Jericho every day. This was an unusual situation, not a daily occurrence. We have learned what principles to operate on for daily living; but when we have a major confrontation in our life, a special obstacle that we have to face, we must spend time with God and discern His will for us in that specific situation.

How do we find out the will and Word of God when we face an unusual obstacle? There's really only one way: Spend time listening to God. So many times when we've got a problem we run to a counselor, the minister, a teacher, a missionary, or someone else. Maybe we go to some other layman who we feel is a little more spiritual. We sit down together and we say, "Now, look, I have this tremendous problem, and I don't know what to do."

This is one way to obtain answers, because if Christ is indwelling the other person and you know He's working in that person, God can speak to you through that individual. However, the Lord will also speak to us most basically and definitely alone, in His presence.

Listen to God

One reason why there's so much confusion among Christians today, even sincere Christians, people who are straight on doctrine and who love God and the Bible, is because we don't spend enough time listening to God. We listen to the news commentator and we read dozens of magazines. But when do we take the time to seek the Lord's counsel?

We find it very easy to spend an hour watching the news, and I don't like to miss it myself. I try to get my wife to fix dinner so that it's either before or after the news. And it's only right. We should know what's going on in the world. We should listen to these commentators, we should read the best writers, but when do we listen to God? How on earth can we expect God to speak to us if we don't give Him time? How can we know what He's thinking? How can we know how to accomplish our jobs?

"Will God actually speak to me?" you ask. "Will God actually lead me? Will God show me the way to take on these special opportunities?" Of course He will. Otherwise, what do we mean when we say we have a personal relationship with Jesus Christ? It's all empty theory if we don't communicate with Him. If we really know Him, of course He's going to speak to us. If He's occupying my personality, of course He's eager to lead me.

In the New Testament we read, "Ask, and it will be given you; seek, and you will find; knock, and it will be opened to you." What does it mean, if not that God is most eager for us to talk to Him, to ask, to know, and to seek His response. He will show us, and He will open the door. But we take so little time with God that He doesn't have a chance to speak to us.

We quote men: "Well, Dr. So-and-So says that this is the answer to world evangelism. Dr. So-and-So says it's the other, and this other person says this. I'm confused! I'd like to pitch in with So-and-So, and yet I'd like to get in with the other man—but I'm not sure." Maybe any one of these three ways is God's way for those particular people. But what about you and me? How are you going to fight your Jericho? How am I going to take on the city that God tells me to take on? I've got to find out from Him. If I'm going to listen to men, I will become confused; but God has answers for all of us.

I was on a plane, going from Miami to Mexico City recently. I sat beside a Cuban-American, who had been in the States for ten years. His father brought him over when he was a boy, when people first began fleeing Communism. He's an American now, educated at Miami University.

We talked about Billy Graham and about Nixon, and finally we talked about the Lord. He told me, "You know, to me there's one word that describes the U.S. right now, and it also describes me."

"What's that?" I asked.

"Confusion," he said. "I listen to Nixon, and I'm convinced he's right. The commentators come on, and they shake me all up. I read one of the columnists and he puts me straight again; then I read another editor and I'm mixed up again. Everyone I talk to is confused."

It's true. Many are confused. We try all kinds of methods to do God's work and to live our lives; yet we're still confused, often living on the edge of panic. We wonder about our kids, and what's going to happen to the church, and so on. These perplexities were not meant to bring us to despair. They were rather meant to bring us to our Father so that we might pour out our hopes and fears and dreams into His loving hands.

DON'T TALK SO MUCH

There's another area to consider in listening to God speak. Notice in verse 10 where the Lord commands the people, "You shall not shout or let your voice be heard, neither shall any word go out of your mouth, until the day I bid you shout; then you shall shout."

Can you imagine asking a million and a half Israelites to keep quiet? Can you imagine that? They were simply supposed to keep their mouths shut and walk around the city.

Silence before God! What a rare commodity! How difficult this is to achieve. If we're not speaking verbally, then there are a thousand mental voices inside our thoughts, each vying for the last word. Listen to God? How can He possibly get a word in edgewise? This passage seems to be saying, "Hush. Don't talk so much. Be quiet before the Lord after you've poured out your heart to him. Let God speak."

Most often (and I'm guilty of this too) we feel that when a person comes with a question, we're obligated to give him an answer. Every time.

But lately, especially after studying Joshua, I've come to the place where I don't give answers so glibly and readily. A person says, "Well, what do you think about this or that?" In the old days I would say, "Well, let's see, why don't you do this and this and this and this."

The Lord said, "Walk around the city and shut your mouth." Why? Think a little bit. Don't be so quick to talk. Everybody wants to talk, but few people want to listen. The first thing is, listen to Him and keep quiet.

The Lord seemed to be saying to His people, "O Israel, my children. There will come a moment to raise your voices. There will come a moment to shout. But just now, be silent before Me. Walk around these ancient walls—this barrier to the land I have given you. Walk and fix your eyes on My ark that goes before you. Soon the walls will crumble like sand before the wind—then you will shout! But for now—just for now—peace. Obedience. Trust Me."

Throughout Scripture you find this advice, "Wait on the Lord." Keep still, wait on Him, wait, wait, wait. But in our computerized society, we say, "Let's go, let's go. Listen to the Lord? I don't have time to listen. I'm thirty-five, going on forty-five. I'll soon be middle-aged. I'm going to die before you know it. I don't have time to listen to Him. I'm going to take on Latin America and win a million and a half people to Christ. The Lord will have to bless, whatever I do." So we charge ahead— straight into the wall—and get nowhere! We fall back, bruised, broken, and dazed and we wonder why.

THE SECOND RULE—OBEY

The second principle is very simple and obvious. The children of Israel were supposed to obey the will and Word of God implicitly. All that the Lord required of them was simply to do what He told them to do. Isn't that simple? We complicate our lives so much. We make it so difficult for ourselves. We scheme and scramble about trying this approach and that approach. We lie awake at night and wonder how it will ever work out.

All that the Lord asked His people to do was to simply heed His Word. Now, granted, what He asked them to do sounded ridiculous; but if they obeyed, they would take over the city. And they did obey. Perhaps some of them had some doubts. Some of them probably said, "What kind of strategy is this? Take over a city by just walking around it? But the Lord said it, so let's believe it and do it." What happened? They took over the city. It was that simple.

In the Christian life, with Jesus Christ indwelling us, with the Word of God written for our guidance and with the Holy Spirit speaking to us, directing us and teaching us—we have all that we need. Once we've spent enough time to know what He wants of us, we are simply to move out and do what He tells us to do.

We'll make mistakes, but the Lord is ready for our mistakes and even for our sins. He's made provision for that. But the Lord expects us, as far as we understand His will and His Word, to go ahead and obey His directions.

1 John 2:17 says, ". . . he who does the will of God abides for ever." He that *does* the will of God abides forever. In other words, the person who does what God tells him lives a steady life, abiding—not only in the sense that he lives for eternity, but that he daily draws his very life from the Lord Jesus Christ. He lives a balanced life, not an up and down experience, one day up, one day down. The person who does the will of God abides in Jesus Christ, constantly walking with Him. His life is characterized by deep-rooted stability, hope, and the fragrance of His Lord. Because he's being obedient.

GIVE THANKS AHEAD OF TIME

The third principle we see, as they take over Jericho, is also very simple. The Israelites had to count on, or rest on, God's Word. They had to consider the thing as good as done. They had to shout, in faith, before the city fell! In other words, they had to give glory to God in anticipation—to thank God for what He was going to do before the thing happened.

It's another principle of faith, one you find throughout the Bible. For instance, Romans 4 tells us that when Abraham received the promise that he

116

was going to have a little child when he was an old man—something that seemed extremely remote by natural standards—he had to wait over twenty years before that child was given. Many times Abraham was tempted to doubt the promise of God. First of all, he was old. His wife Sarah was old. Year after year went by and the child was never born. Yet in the midst of the temptation to doubt God's Word, Abraham "grew strong in his faith as he gave glory to God" (Romans 4:20).

Abraham, just like the Israelites at Jericho, heard the Word of God, obeyed it, and was strengthened in his faith simply by saying, "Thank you, God. I don't know why I have to wait all these years for this child to be born; but I thank You and I praise You that this child *shall* be born, because You have said so." The Scripture says he grew strong in his faith, as he gave glory to God.

CLUMSY ME?

The same thing is true if God has told you to do something that sounds like a monstrous, enormous thing—a Jericho in your life. Perhaps God has spoken to you saying, "I'm going to use you to start a Christian Women's Club in a certain area."

"Who, me?" you say. "Me start a Christian Women's Club? Why, I don't even look sharp. I don't feel sharp. How am I going to start a club for these dandy, good-looking, sharp ladies? Clumsy me! I'm going to start a Christian Women's Club?"

Yet the Lord speaks to you and you feel a conviction, the more you think about it and the more you

117

pray about it. "It is God's will that I do it," you decide. What do you do then? You spend time with God, letting Him speak to your heart. Then you say, "All right, Lord, I'm going to start moving. I do believe it's Your will; I know that You've spoken to me. I can't understand why You would choose me for this job, but I'm going to let You do it."

What happens? Slowly, the Lord begins to do it. So often the most amazing things that have happened in the world have been done by the people least expected to accomplish spiritual objectives. I'm often astounded at the things that the Lord has done in my life. I have only had one year of actual, formal study of theology. I'm always amazed that the Lord gives me opportunities to serve Him.

I'm frightened when I have to do something for which I don't humanly feel capable. When Dallas Theological Seminary invited me to give a week of lectures, I said, "Lord, how am I going to go to Dallas? With one year of theology, I'm going to speak to all these doctors of theology and intellectuals at the seminary?"

The letter of invitation came and I didn't answer it for six weeks. Dr. George Peters wrote me again and said, "Luis, are you coming or aren't you coming?" I was asking God, "Lord, should I or shouldn't I?" because it seemed ridiculous.

First of all, I'm an Argentine. My English is faulty. I don't have the theological background. Finally, after praying, I sensed the Lord saying to me, "Go on and speak to them humbly and simply like the Latin that you are, and let Me use you to bless those students at Dallas Seminary." The Lord did it and I was so amazed.

I talked in private with about 120 of the students. We counseled and talked about spiritual things, about God's leading in their lives. That's exactly what they seemed to need, at least those 120. They didn't need any more tremendous theologians. At that point they just needed someone to come and help them a little bit with some personal problems. I was so glad. Now I'm just waiting for the next invitation. I don't know that it will ever come, but I'm still waiting.

The good thing is this: When you're walking with God, it's not really your capability that counts. It's Him! It takes us so long to learn these lessons, because we're so stubborn! We look at it from the world's standpoint. These three principles we've just covered do cut across all the principles of natural reason, don't they?

And, oh, how we go down fighting. *Listen to God?* In this modern age of computers and satellite communications I'm going to listen to God? No. We're activists. It isn't the normal, natural way of doing things.

Obey God? Well, certainly . . . general principles— do good to your fellowman and all that. But to take precious time listening for some kind of spiritual voice with supernatural instructions? Oh, my goodness, how would we ever get anything done?

Then to *praise Him* before the thing has happened? Shades of the Middle Ages! To blindly praise God that He's going to use you? No. It's unnatural. Praise Him after it's happened, yes.

Yet, when we follow these principles of listening,

119

obeying, and praising God before something happens, as the Scripture teaches, we begin to see God operate. It can happen to you, whatever your Jericho may be. You must sit down and spend time with God. Say, "Now what are the particular Jerichos I'm facing? Things that are really bothering me? What are those things that really weigh heavily on me? My children's education? Drugs? Problems in my denomination? Some deep bitterness within my family relationships? A broken home? A broken romance? An unbreakable habit? What is my Jericho?"

Go to God. "Oh, Lord, I don't want to start flailing around in my own strength and wisdom. What do You want me to do?" Find out—the Lord will speak to you. It may be through a passage of Scripture. It may be through counsel with another man or woman who is godly and who really walks with God. It may be listening to a message from your pastor or in a book or on the radio. It may be just sitting there and thinking about it, but the Holy Spirit begins to develop a line of thought. We can trust the Holy Spirit. We must trust Him, otherwise we're lost. We're on our own. "He will guide you into all the truth" (John 16:13).

The exciting thing is that we're *not* on our own. "I have been crucified with Christ; it is no longer I who live, but Christ who lives in me. . . ." (Galatians 2:20a). If Christ lives in me, I can have living fellowship with Him—a fellowship more real than even between my wife and me, because my wife is sitting *beside* me, but Christ is living *within* me. This indwelling relationship is the most intimate fellowship possible for a human being.

STRANGE STRATEGIES

The victory belonged to Israel. But how foolish it all seemed! How ridiculous it must have looked. Can you imagine the conversations God's instructions must have sparked? Try to imagine yourself as an agent for the Jericho CIA, reporting the strategy back to your superiors.

"Okay, gentlemen, I've got the scoop. Here's how these Israelites plan to conquer us. Got your note pads out?"

"Right."

"They're gonna walk around the city."

"Uh-huh. Then what?"

"They're gonna blow some horns."

"Uh-huh."

"And then they're going to yell a lot, and all our walls are going to fall down."

"Hoot, mon! And for this we trembled for forty years?"

Ridiculous! How foolish! There must have been people who mocked them. The guards on the walls of Jericho must have had a great time watching those people go around.

"Hey, what are you guys doing? Ring around the rosey?"

"Let 'em walk. They'll never take us over that way."

"We thought you were going to attack us. We didn't know you were only out for a picnic!"

Remember what Joshua 2 says about these

enemies of God's people? For forty years their souls were melting inside them, waiting for this day. Then when the day comes, the attackers just start walking around the wall! The people of Jericho must have relaxed, and they probably made up all kinds of songs—little ditties they invented and used to mock the Israelites. They were probably the ones who invented "Ring around the rosey. A pocket full of posey. Ashes! Ashes! We all fall down!"

But this was something powerful—this was obedience to God's will. And when God's will is implicitly obeyed, things begin to happen—mighty things.

So often though—in fact, almost always—when God speaks to us and tells us to do something, someone says, "That's not the way to do it." Have you discovered this when God has told you to do something? There will always be an opinionated someone who doesn't take time to spend with God, who hasn't asked God about your project, who hasn't thought about it for five minutes, but who, when you share with him what the Lord is leading you to do, will find three dozen things wrong with it.

You tell him, "I think God told me to go to Mexico City. (This happened to me.) Even though there are problems and there's going to be opposition, we believe we're going to have a real ministry and shake up Mexico City for God."

The first thing many of my friends said was, "You're crazy. Don't go to Mexico, man. They hate foreigners there. They don't allow foreigners to preach. You're going to find that they'll just put you on the sidelines, because you're a foreigner." They hadn't spent time asking God, "Lord, do You really want Luis to go to Mexico?"

Time after time, if God speaks to you, saying, "Do this for Me, do that for Me, and do it this way," you'll find people who, without spending time with God, will feel the freedom to come and tell you what's wrong with your method. Few people come and say, "God really told you to do this and to do it that way? Say, that's exciting. I'm with you. If I can help, I'll be glad to."

The Lord said, in Matthew 5:11, "Blessed are you when men revile you and persecute you and utter all kinds of evil against you falsely on my account." Many times when you walk with God, discern His will, and begin to operate on it, people will try to discourage you.

The folly of the Jericho plan did not appear to be folly when the walls toppled before the shouting Israelites. Even though it had appeared to be foolish in prospect, the children of Israel had reason to rejoice in retrospect that they had obeyed God.

GOD'S WAYS ARE WISE

The second thing we notice about the procedure of their faith is the inner wisdom of it. Why do we call it the inner wisdom? Because nothing could be wiser than to do exactly what God told them to do. Isn't that the way we're supposed to live, to obey Him, to do what He tells us to do and put the responsibility on Him?

Take delight in the LORD, and he will give you the desires of your heart. Commit your way to the LORD; trust in him, and he will act (Psalm 37:4-5).

The psalmist also says:

He will bring forth your vindication as the light, and your right as the noonday. . . . Trust in the LORD, and do good (Psalm 37:6, 3a).

What is that "good"? It is doing His will.

. . . do good; so you will dwell in the land, and enjoy security (Psalm 37:3b).

The wisdom of Israel was not demonstrated by superior military strategy. It was rather demonstrated by tenacious obedience—a refusal to let go of God's instruction no matter how hopeless it may have appeared.

"This is God's way and I'm going to do it God's way. My friends may think me a fool and the whole plan seems senseless even to me. But this is the strategy of God and I'm going to cling to it—cling to Him—no matter what."

THE ARK OF THE LORD

What is the deeper meaning of what happened at Jericho? You'll remember we noted that the ark of the Lord is mentioned several times in the text. What was the ark of the Lord? It was the symbol (and the reality, too) of the presence of God in the midst of His people. God was there. Among them.

It was an actual presence, the Old Testament tells us. There was a shining light inside the sanctuary and it was the reality of the presence of God among His people. Now, the inner wisdom of the strategy of taking Jericho was this: it was God actually destroying the city. As you read the passage, over and over God says, "*I* will give you the city. You just do what I say and it's yours."

It isn't really Joshua that "fit the battle of Jericho." *God* "fit the battle of Jericho." Joshua and the people simply went in after God, doing what they were told. The presence of God in the ark, in the midst of the people of Israel, was really the power that destroyed Jericho. For us, with our Jerichos, the real power to overcome these obstacles is the presence of God in our lives.

Christ lives in you and me. Therefore, I'm not just a weak little human being crawling around on my belly, trying to serve God in my own energy, eating dirt most of the time. *NO!* I am a child of God; the living God indwells me in the Person of Jesus Christ. And when I have to face these Jerichos, it isn't really me facing them; it's Christ who dwells in me, using me for His purposes. I am delighted to do what God tells me to do and to do it the way He tells me to do it. Then watch Him work.

They had to go around the walls thirteen times, so they had plenty of time to think. First time around, they probably thought, "We'll never make it this way." The second time around they may have thought, "What a poor strategy. We'll never knock these walls down." By about the fifth or sixth time they must have thought, "Well, maybe Joshua is right. The One who's going to *have* to destroy these walls is God and not us." And that's exactly what happened.

This is the lesson for us. If we spend time listening to Him and then moving out in simple obedience—knowing that He is indwelling us, that it's not us trying to win people to Christ, that it's not us trying to destroy those Jerichos, it's God—the victory's going to be ours before we know it.

The result will be that by the time we've trusted Him as the Israelites did, when the moment to shout comes, we can shout too. They shouted and the walls fell down. Then all they had to do (the people in Jericho were so frightened by then, anyway) was to move in and take over. "They took the city." How beautiful! What a triumph for God's glory. It wasn't really them, although God used them; it was really God dwelling among them who took the city through them, and His name was glorified.

This is the Christian life. It's us, and yet it really isn't us. It's Christ dwelling in us, God dwelling in us, who through us accomplishes His purposes in our lives. When we learn this principle, we are on our way to victory.

Yes, it was strange strategy. Even humorous, perhaps—the Israelites walking around quietly, blowing trumpets but saying nothing. But they took the city. Why? Because they were not trusting their own strategy. They were simply doing what God told them to do. When you do that, time after time, you have a tremendous victory in your personal life.

What is your big Jericho today? Write it down on paper. What are the walls that stare you in the face today? Perhaps it is a project that has been growing in your heart and you haven't told anybody about it because you're just not sure. Perhaps it is a strained relationship with your wife or husband or one of the in-laws. Perhaps you need to ask someone's forgiveness and it just seems impossible to even consider it. Or maybe you need to forgive someone who has hurt you very deeply. Whatever it is— write it down.

Then spend time with God. Let Him draw close to you and commune with your spirit. "Draw near to God and he will draw near to you" (James 4:8). Pour out your heart before God and then wait upon Him—listen for His voice.

That little word "wait" in the Old Testament brims over with meaning. One of the meanings is "to be silent." Tell God about your walls, then spend some silent time in His presence, before His great throne. Move when the Lord says move, and shout when the Lord says shout. Follow Him and never run ahead of His presence.

Then look out for falling walls.

7

The Peril of
False Confidence

Remember that we are in victory land. This is victory territory—the Promised Land. This is the land where God is in control. It is God's country, and it's exactly where the Christian can be expected to live. The Christian who is controlled by Jesus Christ is moving in God's country. God is leading him and controlling him by the indwelling Jesus Christ.

Now even though we are in the land of victory, we still have to grow. We still have to mature. When they took over the land, the Lord said to the Israelites, "I am giving you this land, but go in and possess it." It's as if you bought a piece of land from a realtor, but you bought it on faith. The man says it's a good lot.

"I'll sell it to you for a mere $6,000. You can believe me. It's on the lake. It's a great piece of land."

You reply, "All right, I'll believe you." You sign the check and receive the title, but you don't receive the ultimate good of possessing it—I'm not talking about its investment value—until you have walked around it and made it your home.

The Lord has told the Israelites, "All right, every step that you take in this land is yours." The land is theirs, but they are only beginning to take it over.

Often in our own experience, although we have given our lives to Jesus Christ, there may still be areas that are not under His active control. You may still have a foul temper. Now, you belong to the Lord Jesus, temper and all; but this particular area has never been yielded to His direct supervision—it has never been conquered by faith. A Christ-controlled temperament may be ours by decree and yet never claimed in actual experience.

As we look to the next portion in the book of Joshua, we will examine an instance of failure as compared to an instance of outright sin. There's a slight difference here. Failure in the spiritual life actually is sin; but the Lord deals differently with a person who fails through a mistake or a lack of trust than with a person who commits "a sin of a high hand," as the Hebrews called it—someone who disobeys the Lord openly, deliberately. There is a difference and the Lord deals differently with failures and outright sins.

SIN IN THE CAMP

We will also notice in this next passage that God actually does get angry. In Joshua 7:1, it says, ". . . the anger of the LORD burned against the people of Israel." Everyone wants to talk about God's love. And love should have its place as we think on our God, for we would not know the meaning of the word apart from what He has shown us. But He is also a God of wrath. Over and over in the Scriptures we feel that awesome, holy fire of His anger. You do not play games with God and think He will wink at your sin or overlook it, saying, "After all, you're only a little human being. I'll just let it go this time."

Proverbs 1:7 says, "The fear of the LORD is the beginning of knowledge." God can get very angry and can deal very harshly with sin. Have you noticed that every time God begins a new phase in His dealings with man, He gives us one example in which He deals very harshly with the first ones to commit a particular violation of it?

For instance, in the Garden of Eden, Adam and Eve committed the very first sin. What did God do? He ejected them right away and put an angel with a flaming sword to guard the garden's entrance. "Out!" He told them. "You are cursed; you're going to have to sweat for your food. Your wife is going to have to suffer to have children. You are going to die. You can't fool around with Me." And they were expelled.

In the book of Leviticus (chapter 10), the children of Israel began the new God-ordained manner of worship. The new tent for the ark of the covenant was being installed. God gave very minute details on how they were to worship Him. He told them exactly what kind of oil to burn and what kind of incense to use. But Aaron's sons presented unholy fire to the Lord. They came into the most holy place; and, instead of presenting before God the kind of fire He had ordained, they brought in a foreign fire. They obviously thought, "Now, this is better than what the Lord said we should present." They did it their own way; and the moment they brought this false fire into the holy place, God sent down His

131

own fire and they were killed on the spot.

God doesn't destroy everyone who disobeys and does the wrong thing, otherwise we'd all be dead. But every time He has a new beginning with humanity, time after time, he destroys the first one to commit an obvious sin, to teach us that He doesn't take it casually when we try to play games with sin in His presence.

Remember the Early Church? Everything was going fine; the Church was one; 8,000 people were eating together and working together. No one said his possessions were his own. They sold their land and gave to their brothers who were poor.

Enter Ananias and Sapphira (Acts 5). This man and his wife claimed to have sold their land; and, to show off before the Church, they presented 50% of the profit as though it were 100%. What happened? Ananias fell dead at the feet of Peter. Instantly! His wife, who was also involved in the deception, came in a few minutes later. She also was struck dead for lying. The Bible says the fear of the Lord fell upon all the people who saw this happen.

Now, the Lord hasn't continued to kill every other liar and hypocrite throughout history, otherwise there would be few of us left. Why did he do it every time a new beginning took place? He did it to show that His anger against sin is not a joke. Don't ever think that we can get away with duplicity and hypocrisy before God. Even though God may not send immediate and apparent judgment, there is a death and judgment that takes place in the soul. A certain deadness, an emptiness and a confusion comes into the heart of a person who willfully tries to hide something from God. We'll never get away with it. God and His holiness are to be taken seriously.

Galatians 6:7-8 affirms, "Do not be deceived; God is not mocked, for whatever a man sows, that he will also reap. For he who sows to his own flesh will from the flesh reap corruption; but he who sows to the Spirit will from the Spirit reap eternal life."

AFTER VICTORY—WATCH OUT!

The second thing that we notice in this passage is the failure that was caused by action independent of God.

> Joshua sent men from Jericho to Ai, which is near Beth-aven, east of Bethel, and said to them, "Go up and spy out the land." And the men went up and spied out Ai. And they returned to Joshua, and said to him, "Let not all the people go up, but let about two or three thousand men go up and attack Ai; do not make the whole people toil up there, for they are but few." So about three thousand went up there from the people; and they fled before the men of Ai; and the men of Ai killed about thirty-six men of them, and chased them before the gate as far as Shebarim, and slew them at the descent. And the hearts of the people melted, and became as water (Joshua 7:2-5).

They did not take time to ascertain the will and Word of God on how to take over this little town of Ai. Joshua sent men from Jericho to Ai, which is near Beth-aven. He told these spies to go look at the town. They came back and said, "Easy! Listen, we took Jericho just by walking around it. All one-and-a-half million of us. Just send 3,000 this time—no problem." So Joshua, without bothering to ask the Lord, said, "Let's have 3,000 volunteers; go take Ai." Result? The men of Ai chased them and killed 36 to begin with. Then they ran after the Israelites and slaughtered more of them.

The most dangerous moment for any Christian is after he's won a great victory—a significant spiritual battle. A believer must be doubly watchful in these moments. Someone once told me, "Luis, every time you experience a big spiritual victory, watch it. It's the most dangerous moment of your life."

It's true. You become self-confident—that's the way we are. We forget. Who took over Jericho? The Lord took over Jericho, not the Israelites. The Israelites simply walked around, the walls fell down, and they went in; but it was God who had conquered. Forgetting this, the Israelites also forgot the first principle of battle. They neglected the all-important moments before the face of God—they didn't seek His will. They went their own way, and you cannot have God's power for your self-contrived plan. You can have God's power for His plan, but you cannot have God's power for your plan. The attack on Ai had been the Israelites' plan from beginning to end.

There is an insidious danger that seeps into a believer's life after several months or years of happy Christian living. We begin to use our "peace in Christ" as an excuse to let our guard slip. We throttle down a little. "Surely now I don't have to memorize so much Scripture," we reason. "It's not really so necessary to get up half an hour early in the morning like I used to in the old days. After all, I AM a missionary. And a preacher. Dozens of people come to me for counsel. Why should I kill myself to get out of bed so early in the morning?"

I want to emphasize—*we always reap the consequences of being out of touch with God. We can never get away with it.* If we walk for several days out of touch with God, when we finally come back, we realize how many consequences we have to pay for—bad attitudes with people we deal with daily; foolish little things we've said.

Out of touch with God we write a letter that says something cutting. It hurts and it leaves a barrier between you and another person. You don't realize it because you are so self-confident. You think you're doing everything right; but by being out of fellowship with God—away from that intimate one-ness—everything has the touch of the flesh upon it. Everything has that dirty, stale smell of the old flesh. You may not think so; you may keep up the old, positive "Carnegie" smile, the great old-boy image, the solid handshake; but God sees it. There's something in the way we're designed that reveals a deteriorating relationship with the indwelling Christ. Everything I touch has an unpleasant odor that becomes obvious to everyone. They may not be able to pinpoint it, but they can detect the decay. That lovely fragrance has faded!

What happened when the Israelites became over-confident? They had an embarrassing defeat.

And the men of Ai killed about thirty-six men of them, and chased them before the gate as far as Shebarim, and slew them at the descent. And the hearts of the people melted, and became as water (Joshua 7:5).

These were the children of God. They had taken over this monumental city called Jericho with walls 50 feet wide and 100 feet high. Now they have to run away like children from the men of a village called Ai. What a comedown! When we refuse to spend enough time with God to know His will and His Word for the work that we do for Him, we suffer embarrassing defeats too. Sometimes they're obvious, sometimes not so obvious; but we can feel the sting of failure.

THEY BECAME AFRAID

Another consequence was discouragement and fear. At the end of verse 5 we read, ". . . the hearts of the people melted, and became as water."

Out of touch with their God, the children of Israel became just like the people they had defeated only a short time before. Facing humiliation and defeat, the conquering Israelites became as those conquered. Their hearts were gripped with cold fingers of fear and discouragement.

This is exactly what happens to a Christian every time he walks out of fellowship with his Lord. This isn't referring to how many hours he spent praying in the closet, timed with a stop watch. Fellowship is simply day to day intimacy with the Lord. Intimacy implies harmony. As we illustrated earlier with a wife and her husband, it is a oneness, a warm undergirding unity of spirit that one senses when it is present and senses as well when it is not. For when that undergirding is withdrawn, discouragement and fear filter in in its place.

WHEN PAUL DISOBEYED

The same thing happened to the Apostle Paul. Paul was not perfect—he made some mistakes. And when he disobeyed the voice of the spirit, Paul paid for it very dearly. Do you remember when the apostle was going up to Jerusalem in Acts 21?

> *And having sought out the disciples, we stayed there for seven days. Through the Spirit they told Paul not to go on to Jerusalem (Acts 21:4).*

Some of the men there, filled with the Holy Spirit, came to Paul. The Spirit said through these men, "Paul, don't go to Jerusalem."

> *While we were staying for some days, a prophet named Agabus came down from Judea. And coming to us he took Paul's girdle and bound his own feet and hands, and said, "Thus says the Holy Spirit, 'So shall the Jews at Jerusalem bind the man who owns this girdle and deliver him into the hands of the Gentiles.' "*

> *When we heard this, we and the people there begged him not to go up to Jerusalem. Then Paul answered, "What are you doing, weeping and breaking my heart? For I am ready not only*

to be imprisoned but even to die at Jerusalem for the name of the Lord Jesus" (Acts 21:10-13).

Now, Paul's response sounded very spiritual, but he was in disobedience. The Spirit said, "Don't go, Paul. If you go, they're going to tie you up and they're going to deliver you to the Gentiles." But Paul went anyway, and what happened? He was put in jail in Caesarea where he spent two years with very little ministry. It wasn't God's plan.

There is a marked contrast between trials that God allows us to live through for our maturing and troubles that we bring upon ourselves. There was the time God allowed Paul to be jailed at Philippi. What happened? Even though they beat him and treated him terribly, in the middle of the night he was singing praises to God. Though he must have been terribly bruised and lacerated and confined to the innermost prison with his feet in stocks, Paul knew he was there because God put him there.

To contrast this, do we find Paul singing in the prison at Caesarea?

And Paul said, "Whether short or long, I would to God that not only you but also all who hear me this day might become such as I am—except for these chains" (Acts 26:29).

No, he was there because of his own rebellious disobedience to the voice of the Holy Spirit, and his speech to the king reflects his real predicament— he's in chains. He's not singing hymns now. He is suffering the consequences of having disobeyed the Holy Spirit when He said, "Paul, don't go to

Jerusalem."

But in extreme self-confidence, he had replied, "I'm ready to die. Don't you brothers try to make me retreat." So he went anyway and was jailed for two long, dreary years. When it was all over, there was no singing, no earthquake to deliver him, and no converts. The troubles that we bring upon ourselves are those that come when we willfully and knowingly disobey the will and the Word of God that we know to be true. It's serious food for thought.

THIS IS NO TIME FOR A PRAYER MEETING

Another consequence of ignoring the counsel of God was an *empty spirituality* evident in Joshua and the leaders of the people.

> Then Joshua rent his clothes, and fell to the earth upon his face before the ark of the LORD until the evening, he and the elders of Israel; and they put dust upon their heads (Joshua 7:6).

My, how spiritual they looked. There they lay, flat on their faces, destitute before God. If you or I had walked by, we probably would have said, "Now, there's a spiritual man. These men are really serious before God." But you know, it was just empty, empty spirituality.

You'll notice next the shameful pseudo-prayer that Joshua made to the Lord.

> And Joshua said, "Alas, O Lord GOD, why hast

*thou brought this people over the Jordan at all,
to give us into the hands of the Amorites, to destroy us? Would that we had been content to
dwell beyond the Jordan!" (Joshua 7:7).*

What a pitiful way to pray. Isn't that shameful?
Compare this with Joshua 1:10-11.

*Then Joshua commanded the officers of the
people, "Pass through the camp, and command
the people, 'Prepare your provisions; for within
three days you are to pass over this Jordan, to go
in to take possession of the land which the LORD
your God gives you to possess.' "*

Look at Joshua, the big leader. When he was in
fellowship with the Lord, listen to his language.
The language of faith rings clear and strong in chapter 1. How different from this groveling prayer of
defeat in chapter 7. "Lord, why did YOU bring us
over the Jordan? YOU brought us over to have these
people destroy us. Would to heaven we had never
come here!" Isn't that disastrous?

We do it all the time, don't we? I know that I have
acted in this disgraceful way. But I think I'm growing, learning to realize that when my sinfulness
brings me trouble I shouldn't waste time blaming
the Lord. I just say, "Lord, cleanse me and give me
ten more years to serve You. Forgive me."

But there are many who come to me for counseling who still want to lay the blame at the feet of
God. When they begin to experience the pressure
and anguish which their own rebellious attitude
has brought to bear upon themselves, they cry out,

"O Lord, I can't understand. You're a God of love, but look at the trouble I have to go through. Why did YOU let it happen, Lord?"

They blame God. But it's because they're out of touch with Him. When you're walking by faith, you find yourself praying the joyful prayers of faith; but when you're out of touch with the Lord, you begin to pray ridiculous prayers.

Then, finally, a result of his failure to seek the direction of God appears in the empty appeal with which Joshua ends his prayer—". . . and what wilt thou do for thy great name?" (Joshua 7:9b). He appeals to the emotions of God. "Lord, look at this defeat. What are You going to do for Your name? Why, these people are going to insult You." As if the throne of God is going to be overthrown because of a puny defeat suffered by one of His sinful children!

The Lord gets right to the heart of the issue. He says to Joshua that the sin matter (this is the basic problem) must be dealt with thoroughly. While Joshua is still on the ground, praying this pseudo-prayer, accusing God of bringing them into this land to destroy them, God tells him to get up.

"Joshua, this is no time for a prayer meeting. This is time to cleanse your heart and to cleanse these people. I'm not interested in your accusations, in your fancy prayers, your sackcloth, or the ashes on your face. There is sin in this company and it has to be cleared away before I can pick you up and begin to give you victory again."

When things are not going right and we know we brought the trouble upon ourselves, it's no time to

141

call for a night of prayer; it's time to sit down and say, "Lord, which sin brought this trouble? I want to confess it. Cleanse it, Lord, by the blood of my Lord Jesus Christ. I want this thing cleared before five more minutes have gone by." That's the way to deal with it.

The Lord is very stringent here.

> ". . . I will be with you no more, unless you destroy the devoted things from among you. Up, sanctify the people, and say, 'Sanctify yourselves for tomorrow; for thus says the LORD, God of Israel, "There are devoted things in the midst of you, O Israel; you cannot stand before your enemies, until you take away the devoted things from among you." In the morning therefore you shall be brought near by your tribes; and the tribe which the LORD takes shall come near by families; and the family which the LORD takes shall come near by households; and the household which the LORD takes shall come near man by man. And he who is taken with the devoted things shall be burned with fire, he and all that he has, because he has transgressed the covenant of the LORD, and because he has done a shameful thing in Israel' " (Joshua 7:12b-15).

That's pretty strong medicine. Unbelievers say, "I can't believe in a God who would do that." That's because they know it's coming to them and they're frightened that this may be the truth for them also.

In the very cutting and climactic method of dealing with sin, the Lord is reminding us of one simple fact—sin must always be dealt with radically! You cannot fiddle-faddle with sin. It cannot be treated kindly. "Oh, well," we say, "it's just a weakness, ha, ha, ha."

The Lord says, "Friend, *until you get rid of that thing, you are going to be defeated in the land of victory.* You could be victorious right now. You could take Ai in no time. But until you clear up the sin, don't imagine you're going to enjoy the land of promise."

DRASTIC ACTION

So what did the people of Israel do? They did exactly what the Lord told them to do. It was thorough and it was drastic.

> *So Joshua rose early in the morning, and brought Israel near tribe by tribe, and the tribe of Judah was taken; and he brought near the families of Judah, and the family of the Zerahites was taken; and he brought near the family of the Zerahites man by man, and Zabdi was taken; and he brought near his household man by man, and Achan the son of Carmi, son of Zabdi, son of Zerah, of the tribe of Judah, was taken.*
>
> *Then Joshua said to Achan, "My son, give glory to the LORD God of Israel, and render praise to him; and tell me now what you have done; do not hide it from me."*
>
> *And Achan answered Joshua, "Of a truth I have sinned against the LORD God of Israel, and this is what I did: when I saw among the spoil a*

beautiful mantle from Shinar, and two hundred
shekels of silver, and a bar of gold weighing fifty
shekels, then I coveted them, and took them; and
behold, they are hidden in the earth inside my
tent, with the silver underneath" (Joshua 7:16-
21).

Poor old Achan. It wasn't a filthy, low-down sin he committed. He saw a beautiful robe and thought, "What a fantastic piece of workmanship. Sure couldn't get this at Sears. Why destroy it? I'll just hide it. I'm sure the Lord won't care about such a small item.

"And, ah, look! Here's a small bar of gold. Nothing wrong with gold; it's clean. Of course, I'll give ten percent to the Lord. Then here are a few shekels —not much." But the point was, the Lord had said to destroy everything and Achan flatly disobeyed.

In nearly every case described in the Bible where the Lord has dealt harshly with sin, it isn't some terrible, gross, repulsive thing that brought on the judgment. When Adam and Eve were thrown out of the Garden of Eden, what had they done? Just picked a little fruit to munch on. They weren't thrown out because it was such an awful sin—it was simply *disobedience.* That, in God's eyes, is awful enough. When Aaron's sons offered unholy fire to the Lord, it wasn't something horribly sinful—just disobedience, that's all.

When Ananias and Sapphira gave 50% of the sale of their land, it seemed like a minor infraction compared to the Lord's punishment. But God saw their heart and knew the depth of their hypocrisy and their duplicity.

If there is sin in your life, you must settle it and settle it fast. If you want to know victory in your life, victory in the land of promise, if you desire the indwelling Christ to take over and handle the little things as well as the big things, you simply must deal with the sin in your life—immediately and thoroughly.

Don't try to justify yourself, saying, "Well, Lord, it's a family trait. My grandfather was very aggressive and had a loud mouth. I do, too, Lord, and I know you'll understand. After all, it isn't that bad. Well, I am a little loud now and then and the kids hide under the bed when I start shouting. I'll admit my wife runs out the back door; but you see, Lord, it's in the family. You can't hold it against me."

Or perhaps you are the quietly bitter, cutting, critical, jealous type of person. You cuddle a poisonous envy in your inner soul.

Don't play games with sin. It may or may not be a gross sin such as immorality, adultery, or perversion, but it's disobedience. Don't try to justify it. The Lord wants you to deal with it now.

After the Lord told Joshua what the problem was in camp, you'll notice they moved quickly. Verse 22: "So Joshua sent messengers, and they ran to the tent." Not, "OK, when we have time, we'll go search for the problem."

They ran. It says, "and behold, it was hidden in his tent with the silver underneath" (Joshua 7:22b). They dug up the loot and brought it to Joshua. They laid it before the Lord.

1 John 1:7, 9 tells that "if we walk in the light, as

he is in the light, we have fellowship with one another, and the blood of Jesus his Son cleanses us from all sin. . . . If we confess our sins, he is faithful and just, and will forgive our sins and cleanse us from all unrighteousness."

This is exactly what the people of Israel did. They brought their sin out in the open, confessed it, cleaned it out, and then the anger of the Lord was gone. They could begin again.

"Now we're ready to take Ai," the Lord tells them. They've cleaned out the secret sin and it seems the Lord is saying, "Of course I don't want you to be defeated. You're My children. Do you think I enjoy allowing the people of Ai to destroy you? Why do you think I brought you into this land —to make you a defeated people? No, I want you to enjoy the victory that I have won for you."

The Lord tells us the same thing. Why do you think Jesus Christ came to live in our hearts? So we would be defeated men and women, always stumbling, always losing out, frustrated and defeated like the rest of the world? Is that what Christ came to do?

No, He came to give us victory, to fill us with love, joy, and peace. That's the proof of His presence in us. The Lord tells Joshua:

> "Do not fear or be dismayed; take all the fighting men with you, and arise, go up to Ai; see, I have given into your hand the king of Ai, and his people, his city, and his land" (Joshua 8:1).

The Lord gave them orders. They were on solid ground again—back to where they had been before

146

Jericho. This time instead of sending out an expeditionary force of 3,000, Joshua waited for the Lord's orders.

The Lord told them, "I have a different plan this time." Notice the difference between the Lord's plan and the plan Joshua's spies laid out. The spies said, "Only send out 3,000." The Lord said, "Send all the people." In Jericho the Lord had given orders not to take any booty. In Ai, the Lord told them they could take all they wanted.

Does the Lord change His mind? If He does, it's none of my business why. If He wants to explain, fine; but He doesn't have to—He is God! The Lord has a right to change His plans for my life and for yours. My responsibility is to be so close and open to Him that I am aware of the change and ready to move in any direction He indicates.

The Lord told Joshua, "Stretch out the javelin that is in your hand toward Ai; for I will give it into your hand" (Joshua 8:18a). Raising the javelin before the city was taken was like saying, "Glory to God, He's given us the town. Let's go." This time they experienced a complete victory over Ai—as big as the victory at Jericho.

God restored them. The mistake they made in attacking Ai with the wrong strategy He forgave right away, and they experienced once again the sweet taste of triumph.

Remember the story of Ai, because in the land of victory we may suffer defeat. Even though we have the indwelling Jesus Christ, if we fail to walk by these simple principles of faith—know His will—obey—give Him glory ahead of time—we'll be defeated also.

But when defeat occurs, you can confess the problem, clear it up, and through the blood of Jesus Christ be forgiven. You are then cleansed and can get up and go again, knowing that the Lord will reveal His plan and work through you.

The Lord doesn't discard us because we make mistakes. Glory to Him! Otherwise we'd all be sunk. He doesn't put us aside, saying, "All right! You did it. That's it. You're through!"

Instead, He picks us up, saying, "Now we're ready to go again. I don't want to see you defeated. I don't want anyone chasing My people. I want My people to be victorious, not hounded by Satan or by silly little sins or foolish covetousness. That's why I've come to live in them."

> *I have been crucified with Christ; it is no longer I who live, but Christ who lives in me; and the life I now live in the flesh I live by faith in the Son of God, who loved me and gave himself for me (Galatians 2:20).*

> *I can do all things in him who strengthens me (Philippians 4:13).*

8

The Peril of
the Independent Spirit

"So he led forth his people with joy," says the psalmist, "his chosen ones with singing. And he gave them the lands of the nations; and they took possession of the fruit of the peoples' toil" (Psalm 105:43-44).

Does this mean that the children of Israel were now perfect because they were in the land? By no means! Ai demonstrated that point all too clearly. But they were out of Egypt—the shackles of slavery were shattered. And they were out of the desert. Following the ark of God's presence, they now tread victory soil.

Sanctified? Yes, since they were separated unto God—a people for His own possession. Ai had been a painful lesson, but the cancer of disobedience was checked by radical surgery. Now, there were more perils ahead—deadly perils; so it was no time to relax vigilance, no time to coast. But it was definitely the moment to shout in praise to God their Strength.

As soon as the victory over Ai is an accomplished fact, Joshua gathers all the people together, the elders, the foreigners living among them, the entire assembly, "and the little ones." I like the picture of all the people of Israel being together, offering thanks to God for victory.

They raise an altar to the Lord and worship God together. Jericho has fallen, they have taken Ai, and they're thankful.

THE PERIL OF HIDDEN ENEMIES

Israel is now camped on the inside edge of the Promised Land. Soon after Ai, Joshua must face the Gibeonites—wily, deceitful enemies (see chapter 9). The deception of these Gibeonites would weaken the blossoming strength of Israel. As we read their plot, we immediately think of Ephesians 6 where we're told to put on the whole armor of God that we may be able to resist the wiles of the devil.

What a deceitful, cunning adversary we face! And how he hates us. If we only realized how desperately we need the moment by moment counsel and protection of God's Holy Spirit.

The Gibeonites were next in line for takeover by the Israelites. They were desperate! So they devised a scheme. Dressing in torn and dirty clothing, looking as if they had traveled for hundreds of miles, two ambassadors came to the Israelite camp. In their bags they had moldy bread, further "evidence" of the length of their journey.

"Look," they said. "We've come from a distant place. We've heard of what your God is doing and how He is with you in power. We want to make a pact with you. We want you to promise us you'll never destroy our people."

Once again, without consulting the Lord, Joshua acted. He agreed to their terms, promising them amnesty. The result? For generation after generation, Israel had to endure a painfully infected internal thorn, simply because Joshua did not obey the Lord and destroy the Gibeonites completely when the right moment came.

The Gibeonites are an example of how Satan attacks the Christian, coming as an angel of light, appearing very pious and upright. The story sounds right—everything seems to check out. But there are hidden enemies of the soul lurking behind the deception, waiting to destroy us.

Do you see the strategy of our adversary? The Apostle Paul spoke of the necessity "to keep Satan from gaining the advantage over us; for we are not ignorant of his designs" (2 Corinthians 2:11). We need to be aware of our enemy's designs—for he designs our ruin. When he cannot defeat us by a direct frontal attack, he will attempt to slip in by the back door. When Satan could not defeat the Israelites at Jericho and Ai, he determined to try a more subtle approach. And it worked! Because Israel did not consult the Lord, the Gibeonites became as sand in their eyes and blisters on their heels. They would hamper the purposes of God for years to come.

THE PERIL OF DIVISION

Twenty years go by. The Israelites, brought out of Egypt, done with their wandering in the desert, are experiencing the wealth of their inheritance.

151

They've seen God at work in a marvelous way. The promises of God are being fulfilled. They've experienced dazzling triumphs at Jericho and Ai. On and on they've moved, winning battles, taking over the country.

Then, suddenly, when they should have been truly settled in the land with victory a sure thing, the second peril reared its ugly head: improper criticism—division between brothers.

> Then Joshua summoned the Reubenites, and the Gadites, and the half-tribe of Manasseh, and said to them, "You have kept all that Moses the servant of the LORD commanded you, and have obeyed my voice in all that I have commanded you; you have not forsaken your brethren these many days, down to this day, but have been careful to keep the charge of the LORD your God. And now the LORD your God has given rest to your brethren, as he promised them; therefore turn and go to your home in the land where your possession lies, which Moses the servant of the LORD gave you on the other side of the Jordan.
>
> "Take good care to observe the commandment and the law which Moses the servant of the LORD commanded you, to love the LORD your God, and to walk in all his ways, and to keep his commandments, and to cleave to him, and to serve him with all your heart and with all your soul." So Joshua blessed them, and sent them away; and they went to their homes.

Now to the one half of the tribe of Manasseh Moses had given a possession in Bashan; but to the other half Joshua had given a possession beside their brethren in the land west of the Jordan. And when Joshua sent them away to their homes and blessed them, he said to them, "Go back to your homes with much wealth, and with very many cattle, with silver, gold, bronze, and iron, and with much clothing; divide the spoil of your enemies with your brethren."

So the Reubenites and the Gadites and the half-tribe of Manasseh returned home, parting from the people of Israel at Shiloh, which is in the land of Canaan, to go to the land of Gilead, their own land of which they had possessed themselves by command of the LORD through Moses.

And when they came to the region about the Jordan, that lies in the land of Canaan, the Reubenites and the Gadites and the half-tribe of Manasseh built there an altar by the Jordan, an altar of great size. And the people of Israel heard say, "Behold, the Reubenites and the Gadites and the half-tribe of Manasseh have built an altar at the frontier of the land of Canaan, in the region about the Jordan, on the side that belongs to the people of Israel."

And when the people of Israel heard of it, the whole assembly of the people of Israel gathered at Shiloh, to make war against them (Joshua 22:1-12).

The tribes of Reuben, Gad, and Manasseh were

going back to their designated land on the other side of Jordan. On their way back they built a large monument that looked like an altar. Their reasoning was sound—they wanted to make sure that when they died their children would be recognized as belonging to the house of Israel. Their only purpose for the altar was as a symbol, they said, a testimony that their children belonged to the nation.

Immediately, however, their motives were misunderstood. The Israelites thought these two and one-half tribes were going independent—trying to set themselves up against the Lord. So they made ready for war and were fully prepared to fight and destroy their own brothers. But they weren't merely brothers. Reuben, Gad, and Manasseh had spent a long time helping the rest of the Israelites win the land of Canaan from their enemies. Yet, in one minute, without giving them the benefit of the doubt and instead of being thankful for their help, the nine-and-a-half tribes gird up to go to battle against them.

BROTHER AGAINST BROTHER

What a parallel we see in our lives. In a moment of misunderstanding we stand ready to fight with someone who had been a great blessing to us—with whom we've shared joyous fellowship.

The Israelites sent a delegation across the river to hash it out (Joshua 22:13-18a). They still didn't ask questions—they just began judging these poor, now confused brothers who had laid their lives on the line to help them win the land. The delegation of priests and chiefs began to tell the men of Reuben, Gad, and Manasseh just what they thought of those who were such treacherous enemies of the people of God.

> *"And if you rebel against the LORD today he will be angry with the whole congregation of Israel tomorrow. But now, if your land is unclean, pass over into the LORD's land where the LORD's tabernacle stands, and take for yourselves a possession among us; only do not rebel against the LORD, or make us as rebels by building yourselves an altar other than the altar of the LORD our God"* (Joshua 22:18b-19).

Do you get the picture? Suddenly the Israelites became such self-righteous Promised-Land-dwellers that they didn't even bother to ask questions. They just began to sermonize.

"Now if your land is unclean on the other side of the Jordan why don't you come over to our land, you'd be better off over here where we are. We've got a seminary graduate over here. Why don't you come over here where you'll really get the Word, where the land is really clean?"

This they said to their own brothers who had fought beside them, worked with them, and struggled with them. Together they had been victorious in the name of the Lord. Then suddenly there is division in the body. Brother against brother.

It's always amazing how quickly a Christian can turn around and begin acting like a carnal person of the world. How quickly we can become sarcastic, cynical, and hard, forgetting all the love and the fellowship together.

What peril does this point out to us? The peril is this: that even when we've understood that Jesus Christ lives in us; even after we've seen God give us tremendous victories in our personal life and together in Body life as one; even though we have learned many spiritual lessons; even if Jesus Christ has taken over much of the land; even then, there is one tremendous peril that may plague a victorious man or woman—and that is to disband and begin operating as though one could live independently from the rest of the Body of Christ. Never forget that peril!

> *There is one body and one Spirit, just as you were called to the one hope that belongs to your call, one Lord, one faith, one baptism, one God and Father of us all, who is above all and through all and in all (Ephesians 4:4-6).*

What the Lord is telling the Ephesians in this passage is what He tells us and what He was teaching the people of Israel in Joshua 22.

Even though we are victorious Christians and even though Christ lives in us, there is a constant danger that we will forget our relation to the Body. We begin to think, "Well, I've understood that Christ indwells me; I live close to the Lord; I live a winning sort of life; I've learned how to walk by faith. I take time to find out the will and Word of God and I basically obey it too. I worship Him before the answers come, so that by faith I see great victories in my ministry and my life. But I get along just fine by myself!

We forget the other members of the Body of Christ.

Ephesians 4 tells us to recognize and accept our oneness in Christ. None of us is independent of the other. No one can say, "I can get along without you. I can grow even if you others choose to remain spiritual pygmies. I can do it alone. I've got the Word of God and Christ in me. I don't have to get together with you. I don't even have to go to church."

This is a real danger and another one of those insidious "back door" perils. If you haven't come to that point in your Christian life, you will eventually get there—the danger point. Where you've grown so much and are enjoying Jesus Christ so much and seeing others not enjoying their Christian life, you say, "If these Christians are not going to grow—if they're going to remain carnal, I'm going to run ahead of them. I'm going to grow and push my branches into the sunlight. Let the others hug the ground if they want to. Let God do what He wants with the rest of the bunch." This is exactly what the Lord DOES NOT want!

Of course, we'd all admit, "Yes, we're one in Jesus Christ. Of course, I love the brethren. We're all saved by the same cross, by the same Jesus Christ."

The problem is, as someone has said, "I love humanity. It's just people I can't stand." How true. We quickly say, "Of course I love the Church. I love the whole Body. Even if they are Presbyterians or Southern Baptists. Of course I love them. After all, we'll be in Heaven together." But spend time with them? That's another story! So we continue to separate ourselves from the rest of the Body.

The Lord is expecting that we begin to operate as a Body *in reality as a functional fact*. The first thing He asks is that we recognize that we are one and that no cell can live independently of the rest of the body. If I lose one of my fingers, in about fifteen minutes no doctor in the world would be able to attach it back to my hand. Separate from the body, that finger will die and there will be no way to make it live again, no matter how hard we try to fit it back.

Try as we may, we cannot operate as though we do not belong to the Body of Christ. We cannot live without the rest of God's people. It's dangerous to try.

FOR THE EQUIPPING OF THE SAINTS

Ephesians 4 goes beyond recognizing and accepting our oneness in the Body. In verses 7-11 we're told to discover and glory in our uniqueness—because there is a difference.

> But grace was given to each of us according to the measure of Christ's gift. Therefore it is said, "When he ascended on high he led a host of captives, and he gave gifts to men." (In saying, "He ascended," what does it mean but that he had also descended into the lower parts of the earth? He who descended is he who also ascended far above all the heavens, that he might fill all things.) And his gifts were that some should be apostles, some prophets, some

evangelists, some pastors and teachers (Ephe-sians 4:7-11).

Yes, we are one, but each person also has his own personal gifts that the Lord has given him. The purpose of these gifts is to build each other up—not to glory in them, not to talk about them or make a big issue of our gifts, but to use them to build up the other members of the Body of Christ.

The danger is that when we become victorious ourselves, we forget to build others up. We're so happy with what we've just experienced that we not only ignore others, but we even go as far as the people of Israel did and begin to battle with our brothers and sisters in the Body.

BEGIN TO FUNCTION AS A BODY

Then the Lord tells us in Ephesians 4, "If you are one, but at the same time unique, you're a definite part of the Body. Begin to function so as to build the Body up" (verses 12-16).

This is what Body-life is all about. I need you and you need me. Every one of us in a local congregation, in a Bible study group, needs the other. Sometimes we lose that perspective. The people of Israel lost it. They forgot that the two and one-half tribes had been a corporate partner in their success and now the majority were fully prepared to go to war with their co-laborers.

Many times we do the same thing. We forget that we need each other; that we're not yet perfect, even though the Perfect One indwells us; that our victories are not really ours, but Christ's; that the Lord intends for us to be one. It is not His thought that we merely tolerate one another, only acknowledging one another's existence. Toleration is a far cry from the love of Jesus Christ.

We are to "build each other up in love." If you see in someone else a strain of weakness or a struggle in life, don't sit back comfortably saying, "Oh, poor Joe. He's obviously going through it, but there's not much I can do about it. He hasn't opened up to me, and I haven't been able to figure out what's really wrong."

An expression of true Body-life, true Christian love, would be to go to that person, even though it isn't pleasant, saying, "Joe, I see you're not as happy as you were a few weeks ago. I sense there's something troubling you. I don't know if I can help, but I want you to know I'm available. I'd be glad to pray with you. I just wanted you to know that since we're one in Christ, I just felt something isn't quite right. Can we talk about it?"

We should go out of our way to preserve and advance harmony, oneness, and wholeness within the total Body of Christ, being "eager to maintain the unity of the Spirit in the bond of peace" (Ephesians 4:3). It isn't always easy and it isn't what the flesh, the old man, wants to do. It certainly isn't the way the world operates.

We get comfortable and we don't like to feel obligated. "If I get involved with him and his problem, he'll take up lots of my time. I wanted to go skiing Saturday afternoon. It could take two or three hours to get to the bottom of his problem, to take it to Jesus and to find an answer."

Then too, getting involved makes me vulnerable. I have to let down my guard and expose myself a little, and I have no idea what this person's response will be. He might tell me to mind my own business or something. It's too risky.

Somehow, we forget that members of the Body of Christ are suffering—and, as they suffer, we suffer too, whether we like it or not, because we're one.

Our physical bodies operate much the same. When all physical systems are harmonious, we do quite well. However, when we feel a little sick, things begin to change. I don't have to tell you that the whole body becomes aware that the stomach isn't operating right. When everything's going well, I can hardly wait to go into a restaurant and eat. The body is happy, satisfied, eager. But if something hasn't set well, the stomach says, "No food today, thank you." The hand cooperates, "Fine, I won't lift the fork then." The mouth chimes in, "If you put something in me, I will not chew."

The whole body becomes involved with the upset stomach. The whole body is interested that you get well. We want to be all right, we want to live happily and be strong. We don't like that sick feeling.

This is true when we're walking in Jesus Christ and enjoying His rest and His inherent energy. The more we truly mature, the more we become aware of the spiritual state of other people. Maybe we cannot always converse with them and help them that way, but we feel for that member of the Body. They're suffering and it's obvious. You can tell by the sour look, the strange reactions—something isn't right with this part of the Body.

You begin praying about it. As soon as possible, under the prompting of the Spirit, you quietly move in to help. You think, "I'm not going to sit on the side lines and watch. I'm not going to say, 'Oh, something's not right between Ellen and Marv. Let's see how they work it out.' "

No, you want to be a part of their suffering as well as part of their healing and restoration. "I'm not going to let them go on like this." The human tendency is to stay away from trouble spots. Don't meddle. Don't get in on it. But in the body of Christ, the opposite principle is in operation. When there's a problem and you feel the Body isn't developing correctly, you get involved. Not because you have all the answers, but because Jesus Christ is the healing hand and the Body must function as a unit.

Speak the Truth in Love

Rather, speaking the truth in love, we are to grow up in every way into him who is the head, into Christ (Ephesians 4:15).

Oh, how we quote this verse—it slides off the tongue like a paper airplane in the breeze. It's so easy to quote and engrave in gold on our stationery. But in our heart of hearts we're afraid of this truth, aren't we? The thought of speaking the truth strikes a cold needle of dread into our warm, secure little world. We grow accustomed to being good politicians—smart and sophisticated in our subtle flatteries. We conveniently forget that we are members of an eternal family; we overlook the charge of our Savior to build one another up and speak truthfully to one another in an atmosphere of unfeigned love and concern.

Unfortunately, we're used to being double-tongued and deceitful with one another. The Apostle Paul says in 2 Corinthians 4:2, "We have renounced disgraceful, underhanded ways; we refuse to practice cunning or to tamper with God's word, but by the open statement of the truth we would commend ourselves to every man's conscience in the sight of God."

When there is disharmony in the Body, some sick portion, a brother or sister plainly out of tune, I'm not supposed to become wily and psychological about the whole thing. God didn't call us to be psychologists. He called us to speak the plain truth—in love. It isn't necessary to read Freud, Jung, and Adler and say, "Lord, how would Freud do it?" No. The Lord tells us to operate normally, to refuse and renounce the disgraceful, underhanded ways. Unless God called you to undertake psychological training, don't worry about using the correct psychology, sister to brother or brother to brother or sister to sister. We're a family. Refuse to practice cunning. Don't tamper with God's Word by scrambling to find a verse that will speak to their specific case. It's easy to quote scripture and maintain your "safe" distance from the problem. You can do it with a megaphone from fifty yards away!

I'm not looking for notches in my counseling belt. I don't want psychological "trophies" for my mantlepiece.

"Well, I worked another one out, Lord. I applied all the right principles just like the book said and untied all the knots. Pretty slick if I do say so myself."

No! My only desire as a member of the Body of Christ is to humbly and gently make myself available to George or Betty when I see them suffering and not enjoying their life in Christ. I don't have to work out an appraoch or a speech or a scheme. I should simply speak the truth in love to that individual and let the Holy Spirit of God bring the healing and the renewal of joy and hope. After bathing the situation in prayer, I must go to that fellow member of the Body and speak truth in a context of love.

In verse 25 of Ephesians 4, Paul says, "Therefore, putting away falsehood, let everyone speak the truth with his neighbor, for we are members one of another." But we're afraid. We're worried that the truth will disturb the nest. Actually the truth throughout Scripture is compared to light. Whenever you bring the truth to bear upon a problem or particular situation, it brings everything into the light.

Most of the time, you'll find that when a person sees his problem in the light of the Word of God, he will want to see change—if he's a true Christian— unless he's in deep rebellion against the Lord. I believe most Christians want to walk in the joy of the Lord and in the holiness of the Lord. Most Christians want to enjoy forward motion and deepening spirituality. But sometimes they simply don't know how and perhaps God in His grace may use us to help and encourage them. What a privilege to minister in the holy name of Jesus!

We're in the land of victory. Christ is resident within us. We've seen many victories—big Jerichos and little Ais. There's developing maturity, but there's also growing danger, looming peril. And there is so much land left to conquer—so much room to grow in God's good land of promise.

As I allow the Lord to use my specific gifts and allow others to minister to me, the Holy Spirit begins to operate in power. It can happen among congregations, but it must begin in my heart attitude. It must begin to operate in my home between my wife and me, the children and me. We saw in Joshua 8 that even the little children were in on the victory celebration. There needs to be a oneness and openness from the little ones up to the adults in the family and in the local church.

The idea and term, "Body-life" actually grew up in Dr. Ray Stedman's church in Palo Alto, California (Peninsula Bible Church). I have participated with these believers many times. They've put this concept into practice in a real way and it has been a great blessing there, with repercussions around the world. Just out of one local congregation!

When a problem comes up to a board of elders or any Christian group, many times the tendency is to try to overlook it, "pray about it," and hope it will disappear. However, Rudyard Kipling wrote, "Nothing is ever settled until it is settled right." The only right way to settle a thing in the Body of Christ is for all of us to be involved—to handle it biblically.

Basically, when there's disharmony or there's

something to be settled, it must be done in the whole Body of Christ. This openness and love and sincerity begins eventually to permeate a body of Christians, whether it's 12 people or 1200 people. When you operate in this fashion, it's amazing how you begin to build each other up. Instead of keeping resentments and things under cover, they come to the surface.

You see a weakness, the person sees his weakness, others see his weakness. But there's a love that emerges when it's done in the Spirit. The Holy Spirit begins to melt you together and there's a oneness that we should covet and learn to enjoy.

I need you and you need me. We all need each other. But until we take action and begin to operate this way, it will never happen. We tend to hold back, waiting for someone else to begin speaking the truth in love. If you wait for that, it won't happen. It must start somewhere and that somewhere is with you and with me.

When this process begins, under the guidance of the Holy Spirit, the result is something like a miracle. Joshua saw it. Phinehas and the delegation talked with the brothers across the Jordan and discovered that what appeared to be a rebellion was in fact nothing of the sort. It was simply wrong judgment on the part of the majority—a misunderstanding due to poor communication.

> Then the Reubenites, the Gadites, and the half-tribe of Manasseh said in answer to the heads of the families of Israel, "The Mighty One, God, the LORD! The Mighty One, God, the LORD! He

knows; and let Israel itself know! If it was in rebellion or in breach of faith toward the LORD, spare us not today for building an altar to turn away from following the LORD; or if we did so to offer burnt offerings or cereal offerings or peace offerings on it, may the LORD himself take vengeance.

"Nay, but we did it from fear that in time to come your children might say to our children, 'What have you to do with the LORD, the God of Israel? For the LORD has made the Jordan a boundary between us and you, you Reubenites and Gadites; you have no portion in the LORD.' So your children might make our children cease to worship the LORD. Therefore we said, 'Let us now build an altar, not for burnt offering, nor for sacrifice, but to be a witness between us and you, and between the generations after us, that we do perform the service of the LORD in his presence with our burnt offerings and sacrifices and peace offerings; lest your children say to our children in time to come, "You have no portion in the LORD." '

"And we thought, If this should be said to us or to our descendants in time to come, we should say, 'Behold the copy of the altar of the LORD, which our fathers made, not for burnt offerings, nor for sacrifice, but to be a witness between us and you.' Far be it from us that we should rebel against the LORD, and turn away this day from following the LORD by building an altar for burnt offering, cereal offering, or sacrifice, *other than the altar of the LORD our God that stands before his tabernacle!"*

When Phinehas the priest and the chiefs of the congregation, the heads of the families of Israel who were with him, heard the words that the Reubenites and the Gadites and the Manassites spoke, it pleased them well. And Phinehas the son of Eleazer the priest said to the Reubenites and the Gadites and the Manassites, "Today we know that the LORD is in the midst of us, because you have not committed this treachery against the LORD; now you have saved the people of Israel from the hand of the LORD" (Joshua 22:21-31).

It was a wonderful scene as they all reassembled and worshiped God together. There was warm unity again among the tribes. But that danger, the peril of division, had very nearly brought them to war against each other. They had forgotten their oneness. They had forgotten that the God of Israel was the God of *all* Israel. The rediscovery of that neglected truth caused the wine to flow and the harps to sing once again at the fords of the Jordan.

9

The Peril of Incomplete Obedience

Now the path forks again. You've made one choice—the greatest choice of your life—and it's taken you through the Red Sea to deliverance and freedom. The road stretches on ahead, but sooner or later, a little way further, it divides.

One fork leads up through the hills to the place of promise, while the other takes a wide arc back into the arid lands—the desert place. How many of us have found ourselves on that last fork? We went charging with a shout through the ocean, running on ahead, conquering some enemies; but before we knew it, we'd grown careless. Before we knew what was happening, we'd run out of gas in the middle of some ghost town on the edge of nowhere.

Actually a Christian can understand the fulness of Jesus Christ, live for a while in the territory of promise, and yet, if he isn't alert, if he doesn't steadfastly day after day trust the indwelling Christ and move forward, discover that his trail has arched right back into the wilderness.

This is what happened to Israel. It didn't take long. The Lord eventually threw them out of the land of Canaan and made them slaves again. He sent them to Babylon in bondage. To this day, they're still spread out all over the world, because they didn't walk with God and obey Him completely.

A long time afterward, when the LORD had given rest to Israel from all their enemies round about, and Joshua was old and well advanced in years, Joshua summoned all Israel, their elders and heads, their judges and officers, and said to them, "I am now old and well advanced in years; and you have seen all that the LORD your God has done to all these nations for your sake, for it is the LORD your God who has fought for you.

"Behold, I have allotted to you as an inheritance for your tribes those nations that remain, along with all the nations that I have already cut off, from the Jordan to the Great Sea in the west. The LORD your God will push them back before you, and drive them out of your sight; and you shall possess their land, as the LORD your God promised you.

"Therefore be very steadfast to keep and do all that is written in the book of the law of Moses, turning aside from it neither to the right hand nor to the left, that you may not be mixed with these nations left here among you, or make mention of the names of their gods, or swear by them, or serve them, or bow down yourselves to them, but cleave to the LORD your God as you have done to this day.

"For the LORD has driven out before you great and strong nations; and as for you, no man has been able to withstand you to this day. One man of you puts to flight a thousand, since it is the LORD your God who fights for you, as he promised you" (Joshua 23:1-10).

This passage, as you have noticed, is a call from Joshua in the name of God. It is very powerful. The point he's making here is this: "All right. The Lord has brought you all this way. You've grown; you've matured. You've overcome many enemies. There's still some remnant of the enemy to be destroyed, but basically you have rest."

The Lord says the same to us. He's taken over in our lives and, as we've learned to trust Him, we are experiencing a good measure of rest. There are still some enemies and problems to be dealt with, and they'll always be present; but we do have rest.

FOLLOW THROUGH

But there's more. "You must follow through on your obedience to Him," Joshua says. It isn't enough to be at rest. One doesn't simply sit back and say, "I've discovered the life in Christ. Ah, I'm resting in the indwelling Christ. Now I can sort of float along, till the Lord comes in the clouds. I can just coast into glory." This attitude can be dangerous.

So then, there remains a sabbath rest for the people of God; for whoever enters God's rest also ceases from his labors as God did from his. Let us therefore strive to enter that rest, that no one fall by the same sort of disobedience. For the word of God is living and active, sharper than any two-edged sword, piercing to the division of soul and spirit, of joints and marrow, and discerning the thoughts and intentions of the heart (Hebrews 4:9-12).

Many Christians have a real grip on the fact that the Lord of Glory lives in their spirit and for a few years they walk daily with God, spending time with Him in prayer and in the Scriptures, trusting Him and winning souls. Then, one day, you happen to casually ask, "How's so-and-so doing?"

"Oh, didn't you hear? His wife divorced him."

"I can't believe it! You mean to tell me—Frank, my good old buddy. . . ."

I'm amazed at the things that I find out after being away from an area for some time. I hardly dare ask any more. Oh, the sorry things that can happen to you and to me if we forget that the secret of living in the Promised Land is to *daily* trust the indwelling Christ. If ever we imagine that we've arrived and now that we've experienced "Christ in us" we can somehow relax, defeat can happen to me and to you because God has no favorites. Though He loves us all, He has laid down the rules. The rules are that we are to walk daily in the power of our Lord Jesus Christ.

While we do that, there is no danger really. There will be attacks, but we don't have to be afraid. But should we cease to depend on the empowering presence of God's Son, defeat, temptation, and manifold problems may overpower us before we know what happened. Temptation, the Satanic dart that hits you from where you least expect it, will strike ever so quickly when the defenses are carelessly maintained.

WHAT MIGHT HAVE BEEN—WHAT CAN BE

The children of Israel had the rest of the land before them. All the enemies were not driven out, by any means. I often wonder what would have happened if the Israelites had really believed God and kept moving forward in His power. It might have changed the course of history.

For instance, they never did drive out the Philistines and those people bled the Israelites up to David's time and beyond.

All the land was theirs, yet they chose to cast their tents in a vacant lot and stay within small boundaries. They chose to obey God on a partial basis, not cleaning out the entire country but being satisfied to merely dust the surface, so to speak.

Do you realize—have you really considered the fact that we have the same powerful God as the Israelites had? As we face the next ten years, as the Lord gives us life, what are we going to do with that decade? We've discovered the wonderful experience for ourselves that the Lord Jesus lives within us. We are out of Egypt (the world). We've come in off the desert, and now we live in the Promised Land (victory). But what are we going to do with this life? We live in a day of confusion. Even Christians are confused. The job that the Lord has given us—and it's a job that must flow out of our victory in Christ—is the job of evangelism, worldwide evangelization in our day.

Perhaps this will be the last decade before the Lord comes, before the rapture of His Church. The evidences point to that being true. The "times-of-the-Gentiles" seems to be drawing to an end. Within our grasp today are the means by which the Gospel can now be preached to every man, woman, and child in the world. It's an exciting day—"the gun lap."

Shall we be obedient to God and fully finish the task He has laid before us, or shall we content ourselves with partial obedience? That was the great peril and failure of God's people, as we see in Joshua 23.

We must move forward in evangelism. Not with our fists clenched, going out to evangelize those souls merely because the Lord said so. No! We move forward in the joyous realization that the Christ who has transfused our very lives is the Christ who yearns for the children of men across the face of our planet.

WHAT WILL WE SEE IN THE NEXT TEN YEARS?

We are seeing even today a miraculous, multiplying harvest in Latin America, in Africa, in Asia. A fresh wind of God's Spirit is sweeping across the "Old World" European countries as well. Perhaps the Lord will move on the United States again and we'll see many more multitudes of people coming to Christ. It is happening.

The Holy Spirit is lifting up Jesus Christ across the world today. We need to realize that in spite of all the turmoil we read about every day, the world is being touched by God in many areas in a powerful way. In Latin America, in the Spanish-speaking world, the kinds of things that caused the USA trouble in the late sixties are the very things that we have lived with all our lives. Ever since I was a child in Argentina, I've seen revolutions occur constantly. Off and on. One day they may have an election and two years later you hear a strange voice on the radio news saying, "The armed forces, in an effort to bring back constitutional order, have been forced to. . . ."

Revolutions are a repeating rhythm in Latin America. Not that that is ideal, but I point it out so you can realize that God is at work, even in the midst of the revolutions. Nothing halts Him. God is bringing people to Himself as individuals and families are being converted every day. Sometimes these new Latin believers are even more open in their confession of Christ in a revolutionary atmosphere because the things in which one usually puts trust—banks, safety, jobs, security, income—mean little or nothing. You never know what will happen next.

Governments change overnight. A large percentage of government employees lose their jobs and a whole new group comes in. At the next revolution, another group comes in and these move out. The persistent insecurity leads people to look to the Rock of Ages—the One who is the same yesterday, today, and forever. Sometimes the biggest harvest of people coming to Jesus Christ takes place in a land of turmoil and strife. We must not imagine that when there is trouble on the political and social fronts, that God has stopped working in people's lives. Not at all!

REVIVAL IN THE CHURCH

The second thing I believe we will see in the next ten years is an awakening, a revival within many of the established denominations. In many of the Latin American countries there are old line denominations that have been kind of asleep for many years. Lately, however, they've become awakened to God, hungry to discover Jesus Christ in a new and living way. And great growth is taking place! God is bringing people back to Himself and is shaking slumbering churches. People who showed no signs of life, clinging to dry doctrine, have come alive. I feel we can expect this to happen. There ought to be prayer that God will do the same thing in the USA and in Europe.

Recently I was talking to friends who told me stories of ministers discovering a personal relationship with Jesus Christ. I met one minister a few months ago who had just been converted months earlier. He was so excited! Here was a man about forty-five years old who had been in the ministry for years, now spilling over with the story of his recent conversion.

It's thrilling. The Lord can do it again. The revivals that have happened in American history have always been revivals that began first in the older, established churches. From there, the current shot out to unsaved individuals with potent velocity.

We should be alert to the Lord's leading—ready for Him to use us in this direction. Never give up on the Lord, who is pleased to work in the lives of His people and who longs to revive sleepwalking saints and to set them about the work of His kingdom before time fails and eternity utters a final "too late."

THE SATURATION OF NATIONS

Then, thirdly, I believe that during the next decade whole nations are going to be saturated with the Gospel of Jesus Christ through the use of the mass media. God has put amazing tools of communication at our disposal. Through the wise use of radio, television, newspapers, films, records, books in secular stores, and literature of all kinds, the Gospel message can penetrate into every house, apartment building, office, and business establishment throughout a whole country. Even the most indifferent person in the nation will perk up his ears and notice, saying, "What's going on here? What are these people talking about?"

This is an exciting prospect, and during the last few years we have begun to see this take place. During one of our Spanish crusades in Managua, Nicaragua, in November of 1975, an estimated eighty million people heard the Gospel as it was broadcast from the crusade site via radio and television beamed continent-wide by satellite. Think of it!

Eighty million people reached with the gospel in a period of only four weeks.

At a 1976 crusade in Rosario, Argentina, the radio, television, and literature media had the eyes and ears of Argentina to an astounding extent. Scattered surveys indicated that nine out of every ten people in the greater Rosario area were aware of the gospel message we were bringing.

God is not limited. He could do a work in any country at any time. Our glad duty is *complete* obedience to His clear command. We've seen His intervention many times in Indonesia, for example, when it seemed certain that the Communists were going to take over. Suddenly the Lord stepped in and the Communists were thrown out. Now it's one of the most fertile mission fields in the world. Thousands are being converted. We must trust God that many more nations will be open and receptive to the gospel in similar fashion, if need be.

By faith, we must learn to work *with* the Lord to keep the nations open. In intercession before Him, we need to think and plan and work toward saturating the nations that are open—so that people will become aware of the truth and so that the Bible becomes a book that everyone wants to read.

Obviously, the enemy will oppose this work. The Bible teaches that as the coming of Jesus Christ draws closer, evil philosophies will multiply and gain strength. When the Church is taken out of the world, of course, the tribulation will begin in full force—men will rise up against their brothers, and every dark treachery will be unleashed. But while the Church remains on earth and the Holy Spirit is here, we can be God's instruments to reach people. By the millions.

I believe God is calling people to Himself from all over the world. We are privileged to go and evangelize and find those people. All of us, whether we're full-time preachers or housewives or businessmen, whatever we are, are privileged to go and find those people whose hearts are being drawn by the Spirit of God. It is our privilege to bring them to the feet of the Savior.

Many times people ask me, "Yes, but what percentage of those who come forward in your crusades really follow the Lord?"

I tell them, "Look, I don't know what percentage exactly follow the Lord. But do you know what my joy is? Here are 16,000 people that heard the message. There are many who have come to the Lord and they will be in eternity forever with Him. That's what I really care about. Those who now belong to the Lord, who received eternal life, we will see in heaven—they are in His Kingdom forever."

As a matter of fact, one of the most important ministries of our Team is follow-up. All new converts receive literature, including correspondence courses and Scripture memorization programs.. They will also be able to tune in on their local radio station to "Five Nights With the Bible," the Team's post-crusade Bible teaching program.

As part of our efforts to assure that those who come to know the Lord are directed into a local church, we work closely with the churches who hold "Welcome Nights" for new converts and make every effort to incorporate these infant believers into the local Body of Christ. Many times new local churches are started prior to the crusade, as was the case in the 1976 Rosario Crusade, where forty-six new local congregations were begun in the greater Rosario, Argentina, area before the first meeting was ever held.

One of our greatest joys is to receive reports, years after a crusade, that someone who received the Lord in that crusade is going on with the Lord, attending a Bible School or even preaching the gospel. We realize anew that the Holy Spirit is faithful to follow-up those who have received Jesus Christ; and, even if we do not know all the results here on earth, we know that there is a very reliable record in Heaven, eternally inscribed in the Book of Life.

That's the joy of Christian service. We don't need to be discouraged about numbers and plans. He's the strategist, not we. He's the One who draws up the plans—we're just His servants. If we follow through on what He tells us to do, our joy will be boundless. And this is what concerned Joshua in this challenge of chapter 23. Will my people obey God? Will they follow through on God's plan? Will they be obedient?

SPIRITUAL CHILDREN

One summer at camp I was talking to a fifteen-year-old girl. She told me some of her life, some of the sadness. Two years before, she had given her life to Jesus Christ at camp. Now she was baby-sitting two small children. She had talked to them about the Lord and had the privilege of leading these two little ones to the One who loves children so very deeply.

"You should see how these children are growing in the Lord," she told me. She was so excited. The Lord was teaching her things about redemption, sanctification, the indwelling Christ—and she was only fifteen. But even at this youthful age she was experiencing matchless moments of joyous fulfillment as she worked side by side with her Lord in reaching the people He loves.

The Lord may use some of us to bring hundreds into the Kingdom. But even if the Lord just calls you to bring five or six to Himself—think of it! Five or six people have become the Lord's forever and ever through your witness. Through your life, your contact. This is like summer morning sunshine to the Christian—the very pulsebeat of his life. No Christian is truly satisfied, even if Christ is fully indwelling him, until he has at least one spiritual child.

How many spiritual children do you have? Do you have at least one? It is sad when married couples want to have children and cannot. When a couple marries, children are expected from that union. Spiritually, it is the same.

Until he becomes a spiritual parent, the child of God has never quite received the measure of all that God intends for him. I believe the Lord wants every man and woman who belongs to Him to become a spiritual parent. This is the teaching of John, chapter 15.

If you do not have any spiritual children, why not look to the Lord, saying, "Lord, now that I've understood the union with You, now that I'm walking in a new relationship with You, I want to be fruitful."

The Bible speaks of Christ as the husband and the Church as the wife. We should pray, "Make me faithful this year, Lord. I want to have as many spiritual children as possible. Give me souls that will come to You. I'm going to trust You and allow You to use me in such a way that many will come into Your family by being converted to Jesus Christ. This year!"

Expect surprises. If you're walking in the fulness of Christ, you never know what will happen. We must expect surprises when the Lord is at work. The Lord is a Lord with freedom. He is our Almighty Sovereign. You do not know what this creative, loving God might do in your experience, in your life, and in the lives of others. When God is at work, anything can happen.

POSSESS THE LAND WHILE THERE'S STILL TIME

The thing we call "time" is difficult to describe. All that we can really be certain of is that we continually have less of it than we ever had before. That's a sure thing!

We don't know how many years we have left. I have always dreamed of living until I'm ninety-two, if the Lord tarries. George Müller, that great saint in England, lived to that august age and, when I first read his biography when I was seventeen, I said, "Lord, I want to live until I'm ninety-two and be fruitful to the end."

Yet who knows? The land is before us to possess

and enjoy but who knows how much territory we will be privileged to conquer before we're called home? We've only one life to live, only one life to give to Him, to be used by Him. We don't know when the Lord is going to say, "Halt. This is it for you. Come on up."

With all the strength our great Lord grants us, we must be "redeeming the time, because the days are evil" (Ephesians 5:16 KJV). We must make the most of the time we have, because we don't know when it's going to be over. We need to face that, not in a panicky way, but resting in Him and facing reality.

My mind often returns to the memory of a couple in South America. He'd been working for another missionary organization and he told us, "You know, I want to join your team. I feel the Lord wants us to work together to evangelize the masses."

We were delighted. He was a sharp fellow who could really organize and get things done. Prior to his planned date to join our team, he had an opportunity to go to the University of Michigan and get a doctorate in counseling. He was nearly done with the course.

He wrote often to me, telling about a group of young people that gathered in his home every Saturday night to talk about the Lord. The last letter I received told me, "Luis, when you get to Detroit, call me first thing."

So, when I flew into the city, as soon as I got settled, I asked one of my friends, "Do you have Wally's phone number? I want to call him. He's asked me to come over Saturday night and speak to this group of young people."

My friend's face fell. "Didn't you hear?" he asked. "Wally and his wife were killed last week."

They'd been to a missionary conference and were returning in a small plane. As they neared the airport, the pilot was forced to attempt an instrument landing due to heavy fog. Suddenly he made a mistake and it was all over.

A sharp young couple, with the world before them, lots of potential—and they're gone. Their opportunity to minister has passed. It can happen any time—on an airplane, through disease; the Lord knows our time, we don't. Our privilege in Christ is to keep putting out the Word of God, making the most of the time we have, not wasting a minute.

When we consider what it is to be lost, what it means for a person to be eternally banished from the face of God, this by the Spirit ought to be a motivating factor to move us forward in evangelism. Jesus Christ gives us a compassion— His compassion for the fallen world He died to restore and redeem.

There's a little story, taken from the foreword of a book by Dr. Arthur Glasser, that puts it so well.

One cold, blustery night, Frederick S. Arnot, in the company of another young Christian, went to the tavern district of their home town in Scotland to hold an open air Gospel meeting. (This was in the last century.)

These two youths sang a few hymns to gather a crowd, and then they sought to witness to the assembled multitudes concerning their faith in

Christ. Although their singing was tolerated, their words fell as sparks on a powder keg.

Hardly had Arnot begun to speak when a rival chorus of vulgar hoots and derisive howls blared forth, smothering his voice. He stopped, the jeers ceased. He started speaking again, and again was promptly overwhelmed by a flood of abuse.

And thus it continued for some time. But young Arnot knew and loved the Lord. He was in dead earnest about wanting to tell these men the Gospel by which he himself had been saved. And yet, they just would not let him speak of the Saviour.

Tears came to his eyes, and bowing his head in acknowledged defeat, he turned to go. His associate, another young fellow, equally discouraged, fell in step behind Arnot. Suddenly, Arnot felt a hand on his shoulder. He turned, and facing him was a tall, elderly stranger who looked him full in the face, and then with a warm smile said to him, "Keep at it, laddie, God loves to hear men speak well of His Son."

And this challenge was sufficient. Arnot and his companion returned to the corner, and continued their witness. Their courage somehow touched the coarse crowd, and they gave ear to the message that the two men had to bring.

I've read this account many times, but it never fails to move me deeply—especially that little phrase that the elderly gentleman spoke to Arnot, "Keep at it, laddie. God loves to hear men speak well of His Son." Maybe they won't listen too much. Maybe they will revile or rebel. But God loves it! And God will use it for His glory.

Keep at it! Keep putting out the Word! That young man, Arnot, became one of the greatest missionaries to Africa that ever lived. He opened up whole areas of the continent to the preaching of Christ, just because he was faithful and the Lord used him.

Let's keep at it, speaking well of God's Son, knowing that it pleases our heavenly Father. Even if not one single person receives Christ, God loves it. It's His purpose for us that we keep moving ever forward, trusting Him to use us mightily for His glory, obeying His directions. He has given us a great commission. We must not "coast into glory." There's too much to be done.

Had the Israelites listened to Joshua and followed his God-led advice, their lives and their nation could have been so different! But they fell into "the peril of incomplete obedience." What a tragedy!

Don't you, as a Christian, dare do the same. Disobedience brings deadness to the soul. Obey God and so live life to the full!

> And the world passes away, and the lust of it; but he who does the will of God abides for ever (1 John 2:17).

10

The Taste of Triumph

We find Joshua now an old man, ready to die, ready to go back into the presence of the Lord. Calling all the people together he gives them one last, final message.

"Now therefore fear the LORD, and serve him in sincerity and in faithfulness; put away the gods which your fathers served beyond the River, and in Egypt, and serve the LORD. And if you be unwilling to serve the LORD, choose this day whom you will serve, whether the gods your fathers served in the region beyond the River, or the gods of the Amorites in whose land you dwell; but as for me and my house, we will serve the LORD."

Then the people answered, "Far be it from us that we should forsake the LORD, to serve other gods; for it is the LORD our God who brought us and our fathers up from the land of Egypt, out of the house of bondage, and who did those great signs in our sight, and preserved us in all the way that we went, and among all the peoples through whom we passed; and the LORD drove out before us all the peoples, the Amorites who

*lived in the land; therefore we also will serve the
LORD, for he is our God."*

*But Joshua said to the people, "You cannot
serve the LORD; for he is a holy God; he is a jealous God; he will not forgive your transgressions
or your sins. If you forsake the LORD and serve
foreign gods, then he will turn and do you
harm, and consume you, after having done you
good." And the people said to Joshua, "Nay; but
we will serve the LORD" (Joshua 24:14-21).*

Joshua is speaking to a new generation of Israelites. Only few remain who actually remember coming into the land. These are the children of men and
women who knew what it meant to march out of
the desert toward promised horizons. But every
generation has to make their own choice. Every
generation has to "choose whom they will serve."
So Joshua called them all together and the old war-
rior spoke forth the words of God to the assembled
hosts of Israel.

"Put away any false gods from among you,"
Joshua tells them. "If you be unwilling to serve the
Lord, then choose this day whom you will serve.
But as for me and my house, we will serve the
Lord."

Whom do you serve? It's not a decision to be
pushed into a distant future; it's a decision you
make daily, whether you are conscious of it or not.
It is a decision you are making right this moment.
Life is a process of serving one of two persons.
You'll notice Joshua didn't say, "Choose this day
what you will serve." He says, "Choose this day

whom you will serve." We will either serve the living God who indwells us through Jesus Christ, or we serve our selfish ego, which actually means we're serving Satan.

Whom are you serving right now? Whom is your family serving? Who is the King in your home? Who is the Lord of your family? The choice is yours.

The Lord tells us, "All these things I offer, all the victories that I promise, all the promises I give—they always come true. Now you must choose. Will you walk in the way I have promised to bless? Will you enjoy what I offer? Or are you going to go right ahead and serve those foreign gods? Selfishness and materialism, yourself—and whether you admit it or not, Satan. Choose today whom you will serve."

I wish every man and woman would pause and quietly ask themselves right now, "Whom am I serving? The living God?" Are you really leading your children in the ways of the Lord? Do they know the living Jesus Christ personally? Is He evident and real in your home so that there is no question in your mind but that Jesus Christ is Lord in your family?

Or are you still playing around with sin in your secret heart? Are you still so egocentric that the Lord really has no room in your heart and in your home? You may go to church and sing all the songs, but is He really *Lord* to you? God says, "Choose," and this you are free to do.

TWO CHOICES

For the Christian there are really two times in his life that he must make a serious, rock-bottom choice. The first choice is the one of inviting Jesus Christ to come into your life to take over your life, your family, your home, and your future. That is salvation. That is the new birth, the first rest.

You remember how the Lord appeared to Joshua and Joshua asked, "Lord, whose side are You on? Our side or the other side?"

The Lord replied, "I didn't come to take sides, I came to take over." This is precisely what the Lord wants to do with you. He wants to take over completely in your life, but you must invite Him in by faith. That's the first choice. That's what it means to be saved, to be converted, to become a real child of God. "But to all who received him, who believed in his name, he gave power to become children of God" (John 1:12). That's what it means to leave Egypt and cross the Red Sea, getting out into the desert.

There is still another choice. No Christian wants to live a dry, empty, thirsty, hungry, insecure, unsatisfied Christian life. Not really. Yet thousands do. Why?

Because they haven't made the second choice. We read about this choice in Romans 6:12-14.

> *Let not sin therefore reign in your mortal bodies, to make you obey their passions. Do not yield your members to sin as instruments of wickedness, but yield yourselves to God as men who have been brought from death to life, and*

> *your members to God as instruments of right-*
> *eousness. For sin will have no dominion over*
> *you, since you are not under law, but under*
> *grace.*

The basic lesson of this passage is really the lesson that Joshua was trying to impress on the Israelites. They had left Egypt, they'd crossed the Red Sea. They were actually in the land of victory, and yet they needed to look to their God daily—to choose daily to serve the Lord with all their hearts.

No one serves God simply because he makes up his mind to do it. We can only please God when His Son, Jesus Christ, is alive in our lives, directing us, controlling us, molding us, and leading us.

This passage in Romans 6 points up one truth in particular. When a person receives the Lord, *his will is set free to submit himself to the indwelling Jesus Christ.* A man without Christ sins because he can't help it. He has no power over sin.

A man or woman outside of Christ may not necessarily be an "uncultured" sinner; a person doesn't have to be a prostitute or a pervert to be a sinner. But everything he does is *tainted by selfishness,* which is *the very essence* of sin. Clinging to every good thought and every good work is the stench of self. It is not possible for him to overcome. Culture may enable him to conduct himself graciously, but his heart is still the same. He simply can't resist sin. He's infected with it. His whole self is a sin-centered self.

But when Jesus Christ comes in, His blood cleanses us and we are forgiven for all sin. 1 John 1:7

affirms: ". . . if we walk in the light, as he is in the light, we have fellowship with one another, and the blood of Jesus his Son cleanses us from all sin." Redeemed by the cross, this reborn individual experiences the reality of 1 Corinthians 6:19: "Do you not know that your body is a temple of the Holy Spirit within you, which you have from God? You are not your own." *This living Christ unchains the human will.* The person so liberated is free to say to Jesus Christ, daily, by faith, "Lord, I thank You that You live within me. Today, Lord, I want You to control me. Direct me. Use me. Give me victory over every temptation that comes. Thank You, Lord. Thank You because Your power *is* greater than my temptations. Thank you because Your wisdom *is* superlative—and You live in me. Thank You because the source of truthfulness in my life does not arise from myself, but from You. I can face this day with my head up. I can look at the day with confidence, knowing that You are Sovereign, that You are God, and that You actually have Your residence in me. Lord, I willingly and joyfully allow You to be the Master and Lord of my heart, and of my whole life."

YOU'RE NOT YOUR OWN

That's what He's been waiting for all the time. Ever since you first invited Christ into your life, He's been waiting there, in your spirit, (". . . he who is united to the Lord becomes one spirit with him" 1 Corinthians 6:17), waiting for the day when you would say, "Lord, I gladly capitulate. I gladly allow You, Lord Jesus, to take over. My life is not what it ought to be. I want it to be fruitful. I want Your character to be seen through my character. I want Your life to exude out of my life. I want to be a blessing to people, to be fruitful wherever I go. I want to plant the victor's banner over my temptation and I can't do it in my own strength. But here You are, Lord, as close as these words on my tongue. The Word says so, my spirit tells me, the Holy Spirit assures me in my spirit that I'm a child of God. Glory to Your Name. Here in puny, selfish, blemished me, Jesus Christ lives. Now I can face tomorrow and all the tomorrows yet to come with whatever they may bring. Not because I've got anything to offer, not because I've got spiritual muscle or because I'm so dedicated or consecrated (I could fall flat on my face tomorrow), but I can face things, Lord, because You live in me."

That is true Christianity—the essence of what the Bible is all about! When the Lord saved us, He didn't drop us into the middle of the desert with a canteen and a roadmap saying, "Okay, here's where you start, amigo. Someday I'll see you in Heaven but until then, watch out for the scorpions and happy trails!" No, that's not what He did. He knew full well that if He did that we would wander hopelessly through parched wastes and into dead-end gulches until the day we died. We would be in the same predicament as the non-Christian, on the same level of discouragement and personal defeat.

David, the shepherd-psalmist, knew better. In Psalm 139 he sang to his God, "How precious it is, Lord, to realize that you are thinking about me constantly! I can't even count how many times a day your thoughts turn towards me" (Psalm 139:17 TLB). By His Word, by the encouragement of others in the Body, by the ceaseless witness of His Spirit within, God is ever seeking to move the children He loves in the direction of the Christ who controls — the Christ who gives direction and peace. This is His desire and His will!

DAILY CHOICE

God has made His offer plain and clear, His provision is abundantly and thoroughly available but the day by day, moment by moment choice belongs to us. Will I or will I not allow Him a wide open door to live out His life in me? When it really comes down to "push and shove" in my inner spirit, will it be self calling the shots or the Lord Jesus?

A temptation comes along. I have a choice to make. Am I going to go along with the temptation or will I resist it? I want to resist it, because I know God and He has given me a love for holiness and a hatred for sin. Yet I know I can't really resist it, so I say, "Lord Jesus, here is a temptation. But I thank You that You live within me and Your power is superior to this temptation."

Or, "Lord, here's an opportunity. I don't know how to respond to this opportunity. I don't remember what verses to quote or how I can bring this person to You. But thank You that You live in my life. I'll just let You have Your way. I know You'll remind me of any verses You want quoted. You'll remind me of any arguments You want to give out. I realize that it's not me, but Christ."

When a person makes this discovery, when he chooses this manner of response—this way of life—he can wholeheartedly say, "Thanks be to God, who in Christ always leads us in triumph, and through us spreads the fragrance of the knowledge of him everywhere" (2 Corinthians 2:14).

BY FAITH

This verse is invaluable. And the Apostle Paul begins it all with an expression of praise.

"Thanks be to God," he begins, and that word of praise is an expression of his faith. Remember the huge walls of Jericho? Before the walls fell down the Israelites had to shout, in faith. Before they took over Ai, Joshua had to raise up his javelin in faith. Before they defeated the enemy at Beth-horan they had to help Joshua raise his arms over the field of battle and hold them there as the Israelites advanced against their foes. All of these were expressions of faith.

The first step in order for Jesus Christ to take over in your life and help you with your struggles, is to say to Him by faith, even before you see the victory, "Lord Jesus, this is an amazing truth. I can hardly believe it, it's so fantastic. You actually live in me — You actually give me the power to overcome temptation. I worship You, I thank You, and I praise You that my life will be different as a Christian now. No more side trips back into the desert. Thank You, Lord." That's the language of faith and this language always begins by thanking God for what He has said He's going to do. Then as we thank Him,

He begins to act.

In Christ

The Apostle Paul goes on to say, "Thanks be to God, who in Christ always leads us in triumph. . . ." *In Christ.* The triumph that God gives us is not a result of our dedication, or long hours of study, or long hours of prayer, or from any determination that we make ("I'm going to be victorious if it kills me").

How many sincere Christians say, "I'm going to be a good Christian if it's the last thing I do!" They hear a good sermon, they grit their teeth, clench their fists, and consecrate themselves to the task.

That isn't the way. Yes, there must be the decision to serve Him but actually one must realize, "Look, it's not my dedication or my hours of this or that or the other. It is Him and only Him."

I speak from very sad personal experience of at least eight years of wandering—eight lost desert years. Until you understand that it is *in Christ Jesus* that God leads us in triumph, you'll never get to victory. Though you spend four hours in Bible study and two hours in prayer a day. Or labor all night in prayer. If you persist in resting on those activities of yours as the key it will simply not happen, because the triumph of which we speak does not come from self effort. It comes from Him.

Carried in Triumph

The secret is not that I am a victorious Christian

but that the Victorious One lives in me. Paul said, "Thanks be to God, who in Christ always leads us in triumph."

Do you know what this means? It means that this Son of God whom I worship and seek to serve carries me along in the triumph that is already His.

> *For not by their own sword did they win the land, nor did their own arm give them victory; but thy right hand, and thy arm, and the light of thy countenance; for thou didst delight in them (Psalm 44:3).*

We cannot grit our teeth and say "I *will* be victorious—I will, I will . . ." and really hope to see our desire realized. But when we come broken before our gracious God, placing all our hope in Him, we are led to pray, "Lord, You make me victorious. Make me the kind of person I long to be and that You've asked me to be. I can't do it! I've tried so long. I've prayed so much. I've studied for so many hours. And Lord, I've failed—only You know how pitifully I have failed. But here You are and here I am before You. I'm going to let You accomplish it all for me—in me. Here am I, Your willing vessel."

"Thanks be to God, who in Christ *always* leads us in triumph." This is a promise from Scripture. You'll find it over and over again. The promise doesn't fluctuate up and down according to the message or preacher that we hear. We hear some great speaker and we're on Cloud Nine, our own private executive jet. Just sitting there enjoying the stratosphere. But a few days later we come down with a crash and we're back to crawling like a snail in the spiritual life, waiting for the next big speaker to come to town so we can leap into orbit—so that we can get our wheels off the ground and hit the skies again.

That's a miserable way to approach a spiritual life and it only lasts so long. People begin to drop off here and there saying, "Friend, that's not for me. I'm not going to keep on going to conferences to keep myself spiritual. Either I learn the secret or I quit."

Many quietly give up because they feel, "I must be a failure. Maybe I just don't do it right." What they don't realize is that this evaluation is exactly true. They *are* failing. The point is that no matter how hard they try, until Jesus Christ takes over, they'll always be failing. Because in ourselves we are all failures. We are dead. Crucified with Christ. God never expected us to produce any fruit *of ourselves*. That's why He came to live in us, to make us produce the fruit that He desires.

In Triumph

"Thanks be to God, who in Christ always leads us *in triumph*." Triumph always implies conflict, doesn't it? You can't triumph over nothing. If you've triumphed that means there was a conflict somewhere along the line. We've been looking at much conflict in this book of Joshua. We all have conflict. "In the world you have tribulation," says the Lord Jesus, "but be of good cheer, I have overcome the world" (John 16:33).

We all have it, coming from one angle or the

other. There are risks, dangers, and many tribulations. But, "Be of good cheer, I have overcome the world, and I happen to be indwelling you. Cheer up."

MORE THAN CONQUERORS

Romans 8 tells us, "We are more than conquerors through Him who loved us." How can you be more than a conqueror? We are more than conquerors because in a sense it's not really we who are conquering. It is Christ in us and through us, simply carrying us in victory—carrying us through the conflict. So we are *more* than conquerors. We're the emperor coming in to celebrate the victory. Someone else up front has fought the battle, we just join in the Victor's parade.

This is what we've learned from studying the book of Joshua. We've seen how God conquered through the Israelites time and time again when they trusted Him completely. We recognize that there will continually be battles to face in the Christian life too, but the result is assured. We dwell in a land of rest.

This is the Christian life. A life of fulfillment, of satisfaction. A life of victory *in the midst of battle*.

FRAGRANCE OF CHRIST

Finally, Paul says, "And through us spreads the fragrance of the knowledge of him everywhere." He doesn't say, "Now that you have been saved, let's see if something good can come out of your dirty little heart." No, once again, it's all Christ, through us. He spreads His life-changing fragrance.

It isn't us! We learn so terribly slow and perhaps this is why I over-emphasize this point. You'll hear many sermons and read many books telling you, "pray more, read more, and consecrate yourself." But this isn't something we fabricate. We're not trying to "smell" like a good Christian. Anyone can go to a charm school, learn how to smile and shake hands and chat charmingly. That's very easy. Any non-Christian can do that. Anyone who wants to impress people can do that.

It's easy to learn how to smile, how to tape up the corners of your mouth. But we're not trying to "win friends and influence people" through our own personal charisma. We're not trying to attract people by the cologne of self-effort. He spreads the fragrance—*He* does it.

It's usually unconscious. I'm just going about my business, my work, but He is spreading the fragrance of the knowledge of Christ as I walk with Him during the day. Where? Everywhere. In the house, in the neighborhood, or in the office. As long as He is in control He is spreading His fragrance wherever I go.

What a relaxation this brings to the Christian life. In the midst of hard work, decision making, and pressures, inner rest! That's why the Lord Jesus said, "Come to me, all who labor and are heavy laden, and I will give you rest" (Matthew 11:28). That's the rest of forgiveness, of salvation, the rest of inviting Christ into your life and letting Him take over.

"Take my yoke upon you," he goes on. The yoke indicates that you are now united to Him. "Take my yoke upon you, and learn from me; for I am gentle and lowly in heart, and you will find rest for your souls." That's the second rest. The rest of having Him in control in our life. What a great life that can be.

This is what Joshua has been teaching us all along. This can be your experience as it has been mine for the last fifteen years since God taught me this amazing truth. Slowly, He's been taking over more and more territory and my life has become more and more "a life of rest."

Even though my work increases, the family increases, and the responsibilities increase, the rest is right there because it isn't really Luis Palau—it's Jesus Christ indwelling and controlling this South American according to His pleasure.

Therefore, it doesn't depend on my wisdom, my educational background, or my superior theological training. I may be famous or I may be obscure, a high-level politician or the tenth-floor scrub woman. I may live behind some no-name hills in nobody-knows-where, or a penthouse in Manhattan. You see, it makes no difference as long as the living Christ is the final Authority in my life.

Are you resting in Him today? This is God's way to face walls. Is He winning battles and gaining new glory through you? Perhaps this would be the moment of realization in your life—the moment to shout.

"Don't you know that you are free to choose

whom you will serve?" Paul asks us in Romans. Don't you know that? Perhaps you say, "No, of course I didn't know it." Now you know! You're free to choose whom you will serve. Either sin, which is selfishness; or righteousness, which is Jesus Christ. Whom are you going to serve?

I am asking you, in God's name, will you reaffirm your choice before Him?

As for me and my house, we will serve the Lord.

Luis Palau is president of the Luis Palau Evangelistic Team, an international group of men whose worldwide ministry has as its stated objectives to preach Jesus Christ wherever the Lord leads; to stimulate, revive, and mobilize the church to effective evangelism; to plant new churches; and to inspire and encourage young men to go into full-time Christian work.

For further help and counsel, please write:

Dr. Luis Palau
P.O. Box 1173
Portland, OR 97207